Snakes

By Russ Case

Karla Austin, *Business Operations Manager*
Nick Clemente, *Special Consultant*
Barbara Kimmel, *Managing Editor*
Jessica Knott, *Production Supervisor*
Cindy Weston, *Designer*
Melanie Irwin, *Design Concept*

Library of Congress Cataloging-in-Publication Data

Case, Russ.
  Snakes / by Russ Case.
      p. cm. — (Beginning vivarium systems)
   ISBN 978-1-882770-94-6
   1. Snakes as pets. I. Title.

SF459.S5C37 2007
639.3'96—dc22

                                        2007012729

An Imprint of BowTie Press®
3 Burroughs
Irvine, California 92618

Printed and bound in Singapore
10 09 08 07   1 2 3 4 5 6 7 8 9 10

Contents

Corn snake

CHAPTER 1

Reptiles as Pets

Compared with other animals, **reptiles** (our scaly friends—snakes, lizards, and turtles) sometimes get a bum rap. Lots of people think reptiles, especially snakes, are slimy and want to bite and squeeze people and maybe even use their fangs to inject people with poison. So when the time comes to choose a pet, most people pick animals that seem friendlier.

Green tree python

Take dogs, for example. Dog owners can play and exercise with their pooches, brush their hair, dress them up, and perhaps enter them in dog shows. There are special dog beaches and parks, where dog owners gather by the dozens. There, you see dogs running around, playing, barking, and having a great time. Dogs are loved because they give love back. They may lick people's faces, jump on their owners, and want to be with them all the time.

Reptiles are different. I've never been to a snake beach or a lizard park, where people frolic and play with their scaly pets. Snakes don't jump up and down when their owners come home from school or work. Lizards and turtles don't lick your face to show how much they love you, and I've never seen a snake riding in a car with its head hanging out the window and forked tongue flapping in the breeze.

"Which way to snake beach?"

This is because pet reptiles aren't as interactive as dogs and some other pets are. A pet snake or lizard may not want to be handled all the time, generally won't snuggle with you (some snakes might be willing to snuggle with you for body warmth), and may not respond to your affection (although many will tolerate some handling).

Although reptiles are not usually interactive, they still can make great pets—especially for kids!

Golden ball python

Eight Reasons Reptiles Make Great Pets

If adults at home are not sure about letting a snake into your house, ask them to think about the following points:

1. There are some great harmless beginner reptiles.

2. The risk of injury to responsible keepers is much lower with a reptile than with a dog, a cat, or even a parakeet.

3. Compared with other pets, reptiles are low maintenance.

4. Reptiles don't have to be fed every day (but they shouldn't be starved).

5. Reptile foods are readily available at pet shops and grocery stores.

6. Reptiles aren't hairy, so they make great pets for people with allergies.

7. Keeping reptiles teaches young owners about caring and responsibility.

8. Reptiles are really cool!

Rosy boa

People Really Like Reptiles

Reptiles have become really popular over the past several years. Go to any pet store, and you'll see what I mean. For one thing, you'll find many different types of **herps**. There are even pet stores that sell only reptiles. You won't find dogs, parakeets, tropical fish, or cats there, but you are likely to see many different types of snakes, lizards, and frogs.

Florida kingsnake

In addition to seeing lots of cool reptiles in pet stores, you'll find oodles of stuff to help you take care of herps.

What's a Herp?

Herp is a nickname for a reptile or an amphibian, and it comes from the word herpetology, which means the study of reptiles and amphibians. A scientist who studies these animals is called a herpetologist.

Many companies sell items that make it easy to provide pet reptiles with happy homes. These items include different types of lights, gizmos to keep your herps warm, branches for them to climb on, cages to keep them in, and bowls for their water and food. (You can read more about stuff like this in chapter 4.)

People have been keeping pet herps for decades, but within the past ten years, the hobby has become really popular. I can tell you one reason: it is because of the movie *Jurassic Park*. I don't just write books

Ball python

about reptiles; I am also the editor of *Reptiles* magazine. The fact that the magazine came out about the same time as *Jurassic Park* was really lucky! People saw the movie and loved it, and as a result, many wanted to learn about reptiles and how to keep them.

Dinosaurs are fascinating. Of course, it's impossible to keep one as a pet (even if you could find one, it would be really expensive to feed it!), but many people think the next best thing to having their own little T. rex is having a pet reptile. And although it's great that so many people became interested in reptiles after seeing *Jurassic Park*, there is a sad side to their new popularity.

Young people's interest in dinosaurs often leads to an interest in keeping pet reptiles.

Something You Should Never Do

After *Jurassic Park*, many pet herps were bought on impulse by people who didn't know how to care for them. People would (and still do) see a neat-looking reptile in a store, and they would buy it right then and there. After all, these animals are very interesting, and some are really colorful. Often, however, the animal would slowly fade away because its new owner didn't know how to take care of it. Even today, many reptiles die or end up in animal shelters because people don't know how to care for them. That is why you should never buy a pet reptile on impulse!

If you're a smart, caring owner, you'll have a lot of fun with your reptile pets—even though they won't jump up and down when you come home or lick your face. Reptiles are great pets in their own right. Congratulations if you've decided you want to try keeping them. Now let's take a look at the amazing world of snakes, the reptiles you came here to read about!

Yellow rat snake

CHAPTER 2

The Truth About Snakes

Even though snakes are fascinating animals that many people like to keep as pets, lots of other people are afraid of them. On the "fear-o-meter," snakes rank right up there with spiders and other bugs and creepy crawlies that give some people the shivers. There's even a special word to describe a fear of snakes: **ophidiophobia** (pronounced oh-FID-ee-oh-FO-bee-ya), which comes from the Greek words *ophis*, meaning "snake," and *phobia*, meaning "fear." This is a very common fear. Even swashbuckling movie adventurer Indiana Jones, famous for his bravery when battling villains in scary places, was afraid of snakes.

California kingsnake

In this chapter, we'll discuss the myths that surround snakes, which add to people's fear, then take a close-up look at how snakes are put together.

Snake Myths

Some people who have ophidiophobia are scared of snakes because they think these reptiles are slippery and slimy. This is not true! Snakes are smooth and dry. Some can even give good hand massages as they crawl between your fingers. Snakes may give the appearance of being slippery because the scales of certain ones have a shiny appearance. But take my word for it—snakes are not slimy.

One reason snakes have gotten a bad rap is because some old stories, often religious in nature, have presented them as evil figures. In

The snake's reputation wasn't helped by the story of Adam and Eve.

the Bible, for instance, Adam and Eve ended up getting kicked out of the Garden of Eden because a snake tempted Eve to eat an apple.

Not all stories give snakes a bad reputation, however. The Aztecs worshipped a snake god named Quetzalcoatl (pronounced

Western diamondback rattlesnake

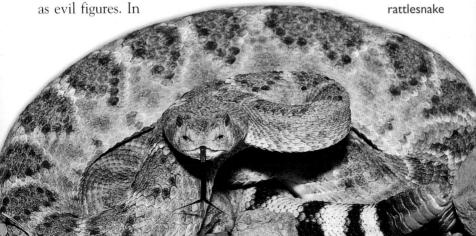

Quetzalcoatl was a feathered snake god worshipped by the Aztecs.

snake, depending on which part of the world you're in) wrapped around a staff is a modern medical symbol.

No Reason to Fear

There have been some pretty odd myths about snakes through the years. One was the tale of hoop snakes, which were snakes that supposedly put their tails in their mouths to form a hoop before rolling downhill to escape danger. Other stories have told of snakes sucking milk from cow udders (the milk snake is a common pet in snake collections, but it doesn't drink milk), snakes with poisonous breath, snakes chasing people, snakes that can hypnotize you, and snakes that will swallow their young to protect them from danger. I even read one tale

ketz-ul-KWAT-il) as the master of life, and the Aborigines in Australia believed the creation of life had something to do with a mythical serpent (*serpent* is another word for snake). Snakes have also been linked by Greek legends to medicine, and to this day, two snakes (or one

Baby green
tree python

Even though a snake may puff up and hiss at you, as this hognose snake is doing, snakes generally avoid attacking anyone if at all possible. They prefer to avoid confrontations.

that says snakes grow beards as they get older! You never know what people will come up with about snakes.

Despite those myths and stories that may say otherwise, snakes are, in fact, fairly gentle creatures. They mind their own business. Yes, they have to eat, and many of them eat living animals. That's nature. This also allows them to perform important jobs, such as rodent control in farmers' barns. And some snakes may be grumpy once in a while. But overall, they're docile animals that aren't out to "get you."

It's too bad Indy and other people are afraid of snakes

Respect People's Fear

You may like snakes and want to keep them as pets, but not everyone does. Never force your snake on someone who is afraid of it, even if you're just trying to be funny. And never take your snake outside where it could come into contact with people who are afraid of snakes. Keep things safe and calm for everyone, especially for your snake, by avoiding these situations.

Some snakes, such as this emerald boa, are naturally aggressive. Others become aggressive through conditioning, improper handling, hunger, or stress.

because the vast majority of snakes are actually quite gentle. If you ever hear people say that a snake chased them, they are probably fibbing. For the most part, snakes just want to stay out of people's way. Any snake that bites someone is doing so usually for one of two reasons:

1. It is scared and defending itself.
2. It is confused and thought someone's finger or hand was its supper.

A cornered snake that's being pursued by someone in nature is very afraid. Wouldn't you be, if a giant chased you, then trapped you in a corner and reached down with giant hands to scoop you up? You would probably defend yourself by kicking or punching or scratching—or biting. That's all a snake is doing. It doesn't have legs or arms so it can't kick or punch. But it does have teeth to bite with, and that's what a scared snake might do. It might also twist its body all around trying to get out of the giant's grip. It might even go to the bathroom on the giant's hands (something you might or might not do if you were in the snake's shoes, so to speak)!

Snakes that are kept as pets often get used to a routine, meaning they learn to recognize that certain events will be followed by other events. For instance, to feed a pet snake, you will have to open its cage, either by opening a door or removing the lid. After you've opened the cage, the food item (often a mouse or other rodent) will be dropped into the cage for the snake to eat. So a snake learns to associate the opening of its cage with feeding time.

A pet snake that bites its owner is often confused and "jumping the gun" at feeding time. This has happened to me. On several occasions, I have placed my hand into a snake cage when my snake knew food was coming, and it was so anxious to get the food that it struck out at the nearest moving object: my hand. It was an honest mistake. My pet didn't mean to hurt me.

A similar accident can happen if you go to pick up your snake after handling mice or other **prey items** (meaning food for snakes). A snake has a strong sense of smell and will be able to smell the mouse scent on your hand. A bite could result.

If a snake bites its owner, it is usually by accident. Of course, if that snake happens to be a gaboon viper like this one, your life would still be in danger! Beginners should never ever keep venomous snakes.

away, and the puncture marks they left behind barely bled.

This doesn't mean that all snakebites are painless, however. Some can hurt a lot. A bite from a big snake with large fangs, such as a reticulated python, can be quite painful. But reticulated pythons are not recommended for beginners such as you, and all of the snakes I mention as good beginner pets later in this book are considered gentle snakes that rarely bite. And even if one were to bite you out of fear or confusion, the bite most likely would not hurt much.

These two biting situations can be avoided. The first can be prevented simply by being careful when feeding your snake: don't reach into its cage—especially not quickly. Just drop the food in and remove your hand, or offer the food using a pair of tongs or long tweezers. The second situation can be avoided by washing your hands to remove any prey scent before handling your snake.

I'll tell you something else: I've been bitten by a number of snakes in my lifetime, and it really doesn't hurt. It's a bit shocking when it occurs because it usually happens very fast; but whenever it happened to me, the snakes always let go right

Hissy Fits

An agitated snake hisses as part of its defensive process. If you're facing a snake that's hissing at you, be wary. Hissing is a sign that a snake is very afraid, and a bite attempt will often follow a hiss. Some snakes are more "hissy" than others are.

No Arms Plus No Legs Equals Creepy

The sidewinder gets its name from the way it crawls.

There are people who don't like snakes because they don't have arms or legs (the snakes, not the people). It's even hard to tell where the head begins and the body ends. This gives snakes an appearance that some folks find weird, so that can be a turnoff for them. Because snakes don't have legs, they have to crawl, and their usual snaky crawling motion freaks certain people out. (Some snakes, such as sidewinder rattlesnakes, crawl sideways, which looks really cool.)

Snake "Legs"

If you think snakes don't have legs, you're right. However, did you know that boas and pythons have the remnants of the legs of the animals that eventually turned into snakes? Look very closely at the sides of a male boa or python, on either side of its vent (its butt), and 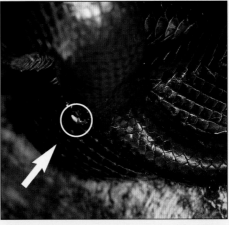 you may see a teeny clawlike projection against each side of the snake's body. Those are called **spurs**, and they're the closest thing a snake has to legs.

Snakes lack eyelids, which gives the impression that they are always staring at you. This creeps some people out.

In addition to lacking arms and legs, snakes lack another common body part: eyelids. Instead of eyelids, a transparent scale, known as the spectacle or the eye cap, covers and protects a snake's eye. Because eye caps are transparent, the snake's actual eyes are always visible. Snakes also don't blink, so they appear to be staring all the time, which I think can give some people the creeps. (The unblinking eyes probably play a role in the myth that snakes can hypnotize other animals.)

As mentioned, many snakes eat mice and other rodents (discussed more in chapter 5). This grosses some people out, and they don't like the idea of keeping a pet that eats cute, furry animals. (They aren't usually as creeped out by reptiles, such as lizards, that eat insects.) Oh well, to each his or her own, I always say.

Snake Anatomy

A snake's body is like one big muscle. If a snake can get its chin over the edge of something (such as the top edge of an open cage), it can pull its entire body up and over. Extending for almost the whole length of that body are vertebrae and ribs. The snake has the standard internal structures that other animals have, such as stomach, heart, liver, kidneys, and lungs.

Snakes also have an organ in the roof of the mouth called a Jacobson's organ. You are probably familiar with a snake's forked tongue, which can often be seen popping in and out of the animal's mouth. What the tongue

is doing is "smelling," which it does by gathering scent particles from the air and bringing them into the mouth to rub them against the Jacobson's organ.

The tendons in a snake's jaw are very stretchy, so a snake can open its mouth very wide to swallow prey.

A snake's colors look the brightest right after it has shed its skin. This corn snake is in the process of shedding.

This is one way a snake can track prey—by following the scent it collects with its tongue.

Snakes don't have ears on the outside of their heads. Instead, they have a bone beneath the skin on each side of the head, and these bones direct sound into the internal ear. Snakes can also "hear" by sensing vibrations in the ground.

Snakes are covered with scales. The ones on the belly are called scutes, and they are larger and thicker than the scales covering the rest of the snake. The belly scales have to be tougher because they pro-tect the snake's internal organs from damage while the snake is slithering along the ground. The scales of snakes can be very prettily colored, and many exhibit beautiful patterns.

The skin is occasionally shed. When it's time to shed, a snake will snag its soon-to-be-discarded skin on something, such as a branch, and crawl out of it, turning the old skin inside out in the process. A shiny new look is the result. When a snake is freshly shed is when it looks its most beautiful and its colors are the most vibrant. If you keep a pet snake, you'll find shed skins in its cage every once in a while.

Then there are the teeth. Snake teeth vary among snakes, depending on the kind. Many snakes have two rows of teeth on the upper jaw and one row on the lower. Some snakes have fangs toward the back of the mouth; these snakes are called rear-fanged species. Other snakes have larger fangs toward the front, which include the hollow or grooved fangs of **venomous** (meaning poisonous) species. These snakes use their fangs to

Bizarre Body Parts

Some snakes have bizarre body parts. A few are shown in the examples below, but there are many other snakes with strange-looking parts.

Cobras have hoods that they can puff out when agitated.

Leaf-nosed snakes have leaflike projections sticking off their noses.

Rhino vipers have hornlike appendages that stick out above their noses.

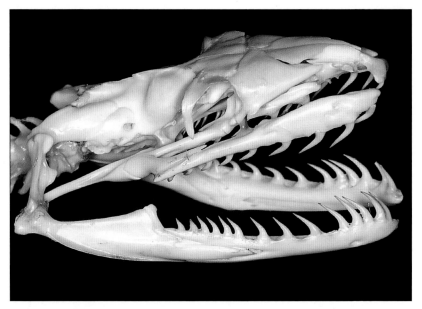

Snakes have multiple rows of backward-pointing teeth. This makes it very hard for prey to wriggle free of a snake's jaws.

inject venom (poison) into prey (or, on occasion, into people who might be bothering them). Snake teeth curve backward, which aids them in getting their food down because those teeth grip and prevent prey from wiggling free. Some teeth are attached to bone; others can fall out (sometimes while a snake is wrestling with prey) and grow back.

As many people know, snakes can open their mouths really wide to eat. This is because they have a unique skull and jaw structure that includes stretchy

ligaments that allow a snake to stretch its mouth wide open while swallowing prey. Snakes can't, however, "unhinge" their jaws to eat large prey items, as some people think they can.

Types of Snakes

Most of the pet snakes available today are either **boids** (pronounced BOY-ids) or **colubrids** (pronounced KAH-lyuh-brids). Many of the best pet snake species are colubrids. This includes kingsnakes and corn snakes. They are widely available in many different types and colors (we'll learn more about them in chapter 6).

Most popular pet colubrids don't get huge. The same cannot be said of some boids, which are the pythons and the boas of the family Boidae. The true giants of the snake world are all boids, including the reticulated and Burmese pythons. Even though reticulated and Burmese pythons are both popular pet snakes, they must be left to the

Eggs and Babies

Some snakes, such as many python and colubrid species, lay eggs; these are called **oviparous** (pronounced oh-VIP-ih-rus) snakes. Others, such as boa constrictors, hatch the eggs inside their bodies and give birth to live young; these are called **ovoviviparous** (pronounced OH-voe-vih-VIP-ih-rus) snakes.

Some baby snakes look totally different than they will when they grow up. Green tree pythons are famous for this. Babies may be orange, maroon, or yellow, but they turn green as they get older. (See the section on green tree pythons for more on this color change.)

experienced snake keeper. Beginners shouldn't even think about getting one of these potentially huge serpents. There is another python, however, that makes an excellent beginner pet. This is the ball or royal python, which you can read more about in chapter 6.

Boa constrictors are popular pets, too, and although they don't get as huge as some pythons, they can still reach lengths of more than 10 feet (3 meters [m]). Therefore I don't recommend them for beginners either. (But you can still read about them in chapter 7.)

Now you know why some people may be afraid of snakes (and why they don't need to be), how snakes are put together, and some of the different types of snakes that are commonly available as pets. Perhaps you may be wondering where you can get snakes of your own. If so, read on.

Burmese pythons may not be big at first, but they will grow huge and need very large enclosures! Because of this, beginners should not keep "burms."

Snake Size

Some snakes, notably various types of pythons, get really huge. The reticulated python, shown eating a pig above, can reach lengths of more than 30 feet (9 meters [m]). (I might add that retics, as they're called, have very large fangs.) Other snakes are super heavy, such as the Burmese python, which can weigh more than 400 pounds (181 kilograms [kg]).

Still other snakes are tiny. The lesser Antillean threadsnake, which is reportedly the world's smallest snake, can crawl through a hole that is 1/8-inch (0.3-centimeters [cm]) in diameter (about the thickness of a pencil lead).

CHAPTER 3

Where to Get Snakes

Where do you go to find snakes? Pet stores immediately come to mind. They are where many snake keepers go to get their snakes. You can also buy snakes from breeders or get them at shelters. Then there's the possibility of buying them online. We will get into those places in a bit. First, let's go to the source—the place where snakes actually live.

Western hognose snake

The Great Outdoors

Imagine this: You're hiking outside on a beautiful summer day, poking among some rocks and scrubby hillside **habitat**. You're enjoying the sunshine and having a wonderful time exploring the great outdoors with your friends. A breeze is blowing, and the air smells fresh and clean. You're hiking along, and there, moving quietly through some bushes, is a beautiful slender creature with black and white bands—a kingsnake! You stop in your tracks, hush your friends, and approach the snake as quietly as you can until you are nearly within grabbing distance. You begin to reach out toward the snake—just in time to see it slither beneath a huge boulder that is impossible to move. You walk back to your friends, who are laughing.

To anyone who has searched for snakes in nature (also known as the wild), this may be a familiar scene. Of course, the snake doesn't always get away. Often the result is the successful

What Is a Habitat?

A habitat is the type of land area where an animal lives, such as desert, swamp, or forest.

capture of a wild snake, and the feeling is great!

Hunting for Herps

Long before they began buying herps in stores, many owners started off catching their own pets. As a kid, I spent hours searching for reptiles and amphibians in the woods near my New Jersey home and, later on, in the hillsides of Southern California.

No matter where you live, wild herps may not be too far away. They may not be right in your own

California kingsnake

A desert habitat can be home to many snakes, including rattlers. Always be careful when you're herping in the desert.

backyard, especially if you live in a big city with more concrete and buildings than fields and woods, but they may still be found within driving distance.

Looking for reptiles in the wild is called **herping,** and it's great fun. There are several ways to go about it. The first is to go hiking in a place where you're likely to find some animals. You can sometimes find snakes by searching woods, desert areas, parks—nearly anywhere that hasn't been bulldozed to make room for

Be Careful!

Be careful about tramping through the wilderness. Always be aware of your surroundings. Never hike in the woods alone. Adults should join in; a fun family outing can be enjoyed by all. Adults can also help you make the right choices about what to wear and take when you go for a hike.

Let Them Sleep!

Some snakes hibernate in dens—coiled around each other if more than one is present. If you come across snakes while they're hibernating, leave them alone! It's just rude, and possibly unhealthy for the animals as well, to disturb them while they're hibernating.

during the winter, for instance, especially if you live in an area that gets really cold outside. Remember that snakes, like all reptiles, are cold-blooded and not very active when they're cool, so they are not usually moving about during the winter. They're **hibernating** (resting with almost no activity), safely tucked away, while you waste your time stomping about looking for them. Spring, summer, and early fall are normally the best times to have successful herping adventures.

houses. The more rural the area (meaning it's not surrounded by houses), the better.

Certain times of the year are better to go herping in than others are. You won't usually find herps if you look for them

Although snakes move about during the day, many seek shady retreats to get out of the direct sun, especially in desert areas. At night, snakes seek out sources for warmth,

"Road cruising" can be a good way to find snakes because they will cross roads at night, drawn by the roads' warmth. Unfortunately, snakes can also get run over while crossing!

including paved roads, which retain the heat they absorbed from the sun during the day. So some people will go snake hunting in their cars at night— this is called **road cruising**.

Certain states have roads that are very well known among snake fans, and they are frequently traveled by those hoping to find some of these reptiles. Unfortunately, snakes sometimes get run over while crossing roads. It's always a bummer for a snake lover to find a snake that's DOR (dead on road).

Of course, many young snake enthusiasts aren't old enough to drive. If you fit into

Always be sure it's safe before you pick up a snake.

this category, maybe a friend or a family member with a driver's license can take you on a road-cruising trip to look for snakes some night.

Or you can take a hike to look for some snakes.

What to Take with You

Before you start hiking, get your outdoor herping adventures off to a good start by buying a reptile field guide. There are several reptile and amphibian field guides readily available in bookstores. (Check out the Recommended Reading section at the end of this book for field guide titles.)

Don't Trespass!

While you're looking for wild snakes in nature, never trespass. You must have permission before entering someone's property. Doing so without permission could get you into trouble, especially if the property owner doesn't share your interest in reptiles.

Your Herping Kit

If you're hiking outside during the day, you may need insect repellent, sunscreen, water, and other gear standard for hiking. Hats and protective clothing, such as long-sleeve shirts and pants, may be needed. Remember that you may be hiking through wild areas that contain plants with scratchy branches. Wearing short-sleeve shirts and shorts could result in cuts and scratches or even sunburn if you forget your sunscreen. Here's a suggested list of what to pack for your day of herping:

☑ Camera

☑ Cloth sack

☑ Field guide

☑ Hiking gear

☑ Insect repellent

☑ Protective clothing

☑ Snacks

☑ Sunscreen

☑ Snakebite kit

Field guides include photos or drawings (or both) of animals you're likely to find in different areas. The books also provide **range** information, often including maps, telling you where the different types of snakes can be found. This will give you an idea of what you may expect to find in a particular type of habitat and in a particular part of the country. This information is especially useful because some snakes have similar appearances. If you find a snake and look it up in your field guide, the range information may help you identify the species.

It is good to check with someone who is experienced in hiking, such as a knowledgeable clerk at a sporting goods store, to decide exactly what to take with you. What you take often depends on how long you'll be hiking and in what type of area.

There is other stuff you may want to take along on your outing as well. See the "Your Herping Kit" box on page 31 for a list.

Some people who look for snakes in the wild take special long-handled "snake hooks"

Never Rush!

Depending on where you're hiking, it is possible you could encounter a venomous snake that looks like a snake that is harmless. Never rush to pick up a snake. Know what it is and make sure it's harmless before proceeding.

with them, which they use to turn over logs, boards, and other objects under which snakes may be hiding. These tools can also be used to pick snakes up safely. (Expert snake keepers who keep venomous snakes use hooks all the time for safety's sake.) You can buy the hooks at stores that sell reptile products or look for advertisements for them in reptile magazines and on the Internet.

Don't forget to take a camera! Not everyone who looks for snakes is out to catch them and take them home to keep as pets. Many people like finding snakes in the wild simply to watch them and take pictures.

Reptile photography is a fun hobby, and this may be something you would enjoy as well.

Be a Smart Snake Hunter

When looking for snakes in nature, it's always best to hike with someone who knows something about snakes. If you do find a snake, don't rush to catch it. This can scare a snake and cause it to defend itself if it can't get away. Snakes will bite if they have no choice, out of desperation. Can you blame them?

As mentioned in the previous chapter, storytellers may lead you to believe that snakes are dangerous and will attack you. The truth is that wild snakes do everything they can to avoid encounters with people. They will often slither into hiding before you see them because they can feel the ground vibrating when you approach. As a result, they can be hard for novices to find in the wild.

Snakes do not chase people to bite them—they "run" from people instead. And if you chase a snake and pick it up against its will, you could be bitten. This doesn't mean all wild snakes will bite, however. Some uppity types may, but other snakes are very calm and will tolerate gentle handling. This is why it's an excellent idea to take along a person who knows about snakes. He or she should be able to identify any snake you may encounter and tell whether it's likely to bite and whether it's venomous.

Rosy boa

Be sure to leave nature as you found it.

Eastern diamondback
rattlesnake

broken branches. Remember: just because you may not see them doesn't mean animals don't live in these areas, and they would prefer it if their homes (even if they're just rocks) weren't destroyed or pushed over as you pass through their neighborhoods.

Don't Break Any Laws

It may not be legal where you live to catch wild snakes and take them home, especially if they are **endangered** species (meaning there are not many of them in the wild). Endangered snakes should not be captured for pets. In fact, it can be illegal to do so.

You may need a permit or a fishing license (or both) before you can collect snakes from the wild. So don't head out until you check your local laws (you may need to have an adult help you with this) and make sure you will be going about your snake hunting the legal way. A good place to start your research is your city's government Web sites. You can also check with your local Fish and

Treat Nature with Respect

Whenever you are out in nature, try to disturb the area as little as possible. Don't trample and break plants as you hike, and if you turn over any rocks or logs, put them back the way you found them. Never litter—always figure on taking home anything you took with you into wild areas. There's a saying that's a favorite among nature lovers: Leave nothing but foot-prints. This means that there should be no sign that you were ever there—no candy wrappers, empty water bottles, or disturbed areas, such as turned-over rocks and logs and

National parks feature beautiful scenery and animals, but it is against the law to remove any animals from them. This is where a camera comes in handy.

Game office. (Fish and Game is a government organization that enforces laws about fish and animals.) Dig around a little, and you'll soon know what you can and can't catch legally.

National parks, which are owned and operated by the government, are beautiful places to observe nature. Some of the most famous national parks in the United States include Yellowstone National Park, in Wyoming, Montana, and Idaho; Yosemite National Park, in California; and Everglades National Park, in Florida. You can find reptiles—and often lots of other animals—in all of these parks. Keep in mind, however, that you are not permitted to capture and take any animal, snakes included, from a national park. These parks are definitely where you are better off just observing and taking pictures of snakes in their natural habitats.

If you ignore laws, you could end up in trouble. At the

very least, you'll have to pay a fine if you're caught breaking them. It's always best to be a law-abiding herper.

Pet Stores

Often a pet store is the first place you'll see many different types of snakes. You may even be standing in a pet store reading this right now. If you look around, you're likely to see some herp cages set up somewhere inside the store and shelves full of reptile supplies.

The better stores can play a big part in your reptile-keeping experiences. Such a store can make all the difference, too, in whether you want to continue keeping snakes. That's a big responsibility, and these pet stores take it seriously. Other stores may be interested only in getting your money, so choose your stores wisely!

Some pet stores sell lots of animals; reptiles may be just one type that you see in such stores. Not far from the reptile section, you may be able to look at birds, kittens, hamsters, or tropical fish. However, shops that sell only reptiles usually have more reptiles and

Many reptile hobbyists get their first pet snakes at pet stores. If you've got a good pet store near your house, you're lucky!

Some pet stores specialize in reptiles, including snakes, and if you've got a store like this near your house, you're even luckier!

more types of reptiles than do the multipet shops, so you will find a wider selection. The owners of reptile-only stores sometimes breed reptiles, too.

Both types of stores can be excellent places to purchase pet snakes. No matter which type you choose to visit, however, there are some things you should pay attention to. Use the following three criteria when deciding whether to buy a snake from a store.

Cleanliness

The store and the cages in which the animals are kept should be clean. Cleanliness results in better animal health, whether you're talking about reptiles or giraffes. If the cages at a store contain rotting, uneaten food or old animal poop—or if they stink—then you should think twice about buying any snakes from that store.

The Animals' Health

The animals you want to buy should be healthy. That means while you're in a store you need to be able to tell whether a snake is healthy or sick. So let's briefly discuss the signs of healthy and sick snakes. (You'll

Pay attention to how snakes are kept at places where you're thinking of buying them. This ball python's enclosure is dirty and too small.

learn more about common snake health problems and how to prevent them in your pet snakes in chapter 8.)

If you see a snake with skin that is hanging in loose folds, then it may not be healthy; chances are it's dehydrated or starving. Never buy such a snake. The skin of healthy snakes looks like it fits properly. If the skin looks withered and sunken in, the snake is not in prime condition.

If you find a snake you want to buy, ask to see it up close. Give it a quick inspection for any parasites (more about them in chapter 8) that may be on it as well as for stuff coming out of

its nose, eyes, or vent (its butt, in other words). There shouldn't be anything stuck to these areas or oozing out of them.

Look also for any wounds, small or otherwise, on the snake's body. The nose can get rubbed raw and become infected if a snake spends all its time trying to find a way out of its enclosure. Look for missing scales, weird bumps and lumps, and anything else that doesn't look normal. Check to see whether there are any dried patches of skin stuck to the snake or shed eye caps still stuck to the snake's eye. (Learn more about these problems in chapter 8.) These could be signs of a snake that's having trouble shedding its skin properly, which can be a health problem or a **husbandry** flaw (cages that are not kept humid enough, for instance).

Sometimes a snake may look healthy but not actually be well. One way to tell whether a snake is healthy is to find out whether it's eating. Ask a store employee to feed the snake while you watch. If the snake is not hungry, come back later when it's ready to eat again. If the snake eats readily, that's a good sign.

It is helpful to know whether an animal was born in **captivity** or caught in the wild. **Captive-bred** animals are usually

Don't Buy a Sick One!

Some people buy sick snakes thinking they can help those snakes get well. Don't do it! You're likely to spend a lot of money on veterinary bills and medicine, and there's no guarantee that a sick snake will get well under your care. Why start off with such a problem? Buy only healthy snakes.

healthier than wild animals are. This doesn't mean captive-bred snakes come with a 100 percent health guarantee, but their

If possible, inspect a snake before you purchase it. Look for skin abnormalities such as blisters and cuts, crusting around the cloaca, and other signs of illness.

This is a typical temporary snake display like one you would see at a snake dealer's booth at a reptile expo. It offers a good view of the snakes that are for sale.

chances of being healthy are better. They are also more used to being in captivity and won't typically stress out the way wild animals sometimes will when they're kept in cages. **Wild-caught** snakes may need more time than captive-bred snakes do to settle down in captivity and may have some health issues that require veterinary care.

Captive-bred animals are usually more expensive than wild-caught ones. This is because it costs money to raise them in captivity. Even though captive-bred snakes cost more, many reptile keepers think the additional price is worth it. See the "Captive-Bred Versus Wild-Caught" box to learn more about the differences between the two.

Not all types of snakes are bred widely in captivity, however, so if you want a particular type, you may have to get one that was caught in the wild. Wild-caught snakes can still make fine pets.

An alert snake that doesn't have any skin abnormalities, is clean, and is eating is a good choice to buy. It's always a wise idea, however, to take any new pet snake to a veterinarian (a doctor for animals) for a checkup, just to be sure there isn't something wrong inside the snake.

A Knowledgeable Staff

Do the store employees seem smart, and are they willing to help you even after you get your new snake home? Some

pet store employees work there because they like animals and know a lot about them. Others just need a job. Whenever possible, it's best to find a store with people who know and

Captive-Bred Versus Wild-Caught

Captive-bred snakes can be great choices for several reasons. For one, captive-bred snakes are often healthier and less likely to be infected with parasites. For another, captive-bred snakes are used to captivity, whereas wild-caught snakes are captured in their natural habitats and eventually shipped to pet stores. Snakes that go through this shipping process can be stressed out, which can lead to sickness.

In addition, by buying captive-bred snakes, you are helping protect the environment. People worry whenever animals are removed from their habitats to be sold as pets; if too many are taken away, the balance of nature could be badly affected.

Albino corn snake

care about the animals. And the staff should be willing to help you and answer questions even after you make your purchase. Ask ahead of time what the store's policy is regarding this and what kind of guarantee the store offers on its animals (in case your new pet gets sick or dies).

Reptile Breeders and Reptile Expos

Lots of people breed reptiles, and a number of them make a lot of money doing so. (I don't know about you, but I think this would be a fun job!) Some of them breed only snakes; others prefer to breed lizards. Some breed lots of different reptiles, including lizards, snakes, and maybe even turtles and frogs. Others may raise only one type of snake or lizard. You can often buy snakes directly from the people who breed them.

Many professional reptile breeders have Web sites you can visit to learn about them and their animals. Some of these breeders post care tips on their Web sites; others sell supplies, T-shirts, and other reptile stuff.

Many reptile breeders don't sell their animals to pet stores. They prefer to sell their reptiles either through their Web sites or at reptile shows. These shows, also called expos, usually consist of a number of booths and tables in a large room. There are big expos and small ones; the big ones can attract hundreds of breeders, selling lots of different types of reptiles. Expos pop up all

Animal Shelters and Rescues

Some animals escape from their homes, and others are set free on purpose by irresponsible owners who no longer want them. Either situation can be very sad.

A number of lost animals end up in animal shelters and rescues, which care for them and try to find them new homes. Sometimes pet owners who can no longer care for their pets, or who no longer want to, will take their animals to these places, hoping the people working there will find new homes for the pets.

Occasionally, snakes end up at a shelter. Most of these are pythons and boa constrictors that grew so large their owners couldn't care for them properly. I don't recommend a large python or a boa for a first-time snake owner or for anyone who doesn't have the ability (including the space for a big cage) to care for such snakes.

Sometimes other types of snakes can be found at shelters and rescues, and if you can provide a homeless pet with a new home, that's great. Keep these places in mind if you want a pet snake (or any other kind of pet), as shelter animals are desperately in need of help. Remember, too, what I said earlier about taking home sick animals. This is usually not a good idea, especially if you're a young herp keeper.

over the world. Currently, the biggest one in the United States takes place each August in Daytona Beach, Florida. Many other cities host reptile expos now and then. Some are put together by reptile clubs; others are organized by professional companies. There are European reptile expos, too. (Germany has some big ones.) You can find listings for upcoming shows in magazines and newspapers as well as on the Internet.

If you've never been to a reptile expo, you really should go. You'll be surrounded by people who like reptiles, and you'll be able to talk to breeders. You can learn a lot at an expo and get a great deal of useful information from many people. At some expos, you will be able to sit in on reptile lectures that are given by well-known experts and participate in contests and other fun activities. Depending on the show, you may see all types of reptiles for sale, including the latest color **morphs**, or mutations (mentioned in chapter 6), as well as old favorites. And there are lots of snakes, of course!

Now that you know where to get pet snakes, it's time to learn about the type of equipment you will need to maintain them properly.

Reptile expos are great places to go look at snakes and other reptiles and to learn a lot about them. They're good places to buy them, too!

Buying Reptiles on the Internet

You can often buy pet snakes directly from reptile breeders who have Web sites. Buying a snake over the Internet is a bit different from buying one in a pet store. The biggest difference is that you can walk into a pet store and inspect the snake you want to buy in person. If you find a snake you want to buy on a Web site, you have to rely on pictures of it and on the word of the breeder to determine whether you really want to get it.

Do some detective work to find out whether an Internet reptile breeder is a good one. You can post questions on the Internet about breeders. You may need someone familiar with Internet chat rooms and message boards to help you. Ask online dealers whether they can provide references (the e-mail addresses or phone numbers of people with whom they have previously done business). Breeders also should be patient and willing to offer good care advice and guarantees on their reptiles.

CHAPTER 4

Your Snake's Home

T he first fact to keep in mind when setting up your snake's enclosure is that snakes are the best reptilian escape artists. Their cages need to be escape-proof. Luckily, most enclosures that are sold for use with snakes include some type of lock that will keep your snake safe inside its cage. The type of enclosure to use and what goes inside are discussed below.

Green tree python

The Enclosure

Green anaconda

There are three general categories of enclosures you can use with snakes: glass aquariums and terrariums, sliding-front enclosures, and plastic containers.

Aquariums are fine for snakes, provided they're large enough. (See chapter 6 for size suggestions for the beginner snakes discussed there.) You can buy terrariums that are sold for use with reptiles; this type may include a sliding-screen top. A standard aquarium, such as the type you would use for tropical fish, can also be used with a screen top you purchase separately. The drawback with aquariums is that screen tops make it a bit harder to maintain

This Mandarin rat snake seems comfy, although the snake should be provided with a hide box to help it feel safe and secure.

Enclosures that have locks are a good idea for snake keepers because snakes are born escape artists. A lock can also keep unwanted hands out of your snake's home.

the right level of humidity in the enclosure, which is something you will need to do if you want to keep a ball python (see chapter 6).

Sliding-front enclosures, often made of heavy-duty plastic, usually have an all-glass front panel that you can slide open when you need to access the inside of the cage. This type of enclosure contains humidity better than an aquarium with a screen top does.

Many breeders keep their snakes in plastic tubs or similar containers, such as plastic sweater boxes or (for baby snakes) shoeboxes. They'll keep dozens of snakes in a rack system that contains the boxes holding the individual snakes. The average **hobbyist**, though,

Always Remember!

Be sure your snake cage is escape-proof. Otherwise, you will very likely lose your snake.

Racks like this are used by professional snake breeders.

usually prefers an enclosure that allows easy observation of the snakes. That would be one of the other enclosures mentioned.

In the Bottom

There are a few choices for **substrates**. Newspaper is often used, as it's very simple to remove and replace when it becomes soiled. The drawback is that newspaper doesn't look natural.

Often used for reptile bedding are wood products, including aspen bedding and cypress mulch. You might see snakes kept on pine shavings, but this is not recommended, as pine shavings can be very dusty. Because the snake will be crawling around in the shavings, the snake could inhale dust, which may cause respiratory problems.

Newspaper may not be the most natural-looking substrate, but it's inexpensive and very easy to replace when it gets dirty.

Cypress mulch makes a good substrate for snakes, especially if the species being kept requires humidity in its cage.

Another product to avoid when it comes to snake substrate is cedar. Cedar shavings contain oils that emit fumes that are unhealthy for snakes.

Sand can be used with some snakes. Use either reptile sand you can buy in reptile and pet stores or playground sand you can buy in hardware and do-it-yourself stores.

Snakes from deserts and dry habitats can live on sand, but don't use this substrate for snakes that require a humid environment. They'll dry out on it!

Artificial turf can be cut to fit a snake's cage. Replace a soiled piece with a clean one, and wash the dirty piece so you can use it when the other gets soiled.

Don't take sand from a beach or other public place, as it may be dirty or otherwise unsafe to use with your snake.

Artificial turf (sometimes called Astroturf) or "reptile carpet" (available in many pet stores) can be used with snakes, too. These are both easy to remove and clean if they get soiled. If you have a few pieces cut to fit your snake enclosure, whenever you notice that the one inside the cage is dirty, you can simply take that piece out and put in a clean one. Then clean the dirty one to use again later.

Something to keep in mind when choosing substrates is whether they could hurt your snake if it accidentally swallows some. Certain substrates can cause an impaction. Read more about impactions in chapter 8.

What Is Substrate?

Substrate is the material you put on the bottom of a reptile's cage. There are different types made from such materials as wood, paper, and sand.

Stacked rocks can provide hiding places, which are important for snakes. Just be sure your snake can't knock the rocks down.

Decorating: Not Too Fancy

Keepers of lizards and amphibians enjoy setting up natural enclosures that contain branches, mosses, rocks, and other objects found in nature. Some snake owners do this, too, but many owners keep their snake cages somewhat sparse. This is because a crawling snake can easily mess up any type of cage decorations in the enclosure. Plants and other stuff in the snake cage will be moved around and maybe even be destroyed. So aside from

Blood-red corn snake

Hiding places allow a snake to feel secure and safe. If a hiding place is not provided, a snake can get stressed out and become sick. It might stop eating, too.

Ready-made hiding places—in the form of pieces of bark, logs, and ceramic containers—can often be

purchased at pet and reptile stores. You can also make your own out of wood, boxes (such as shoeboxes), or plastic containers (such as old margarine tubs). Basically, all you need to do is cut an entrance and exit hole into the container that is large enough to allow the snake to pass through easily. If you're using a plastic container, be sure the hole doesn't have sharp edges that might injure your snake. For containers with lids, you can either leave the lid on or take it off.

To make an entrance hole, take the lid off, and starting at the lip of the container, cut downward, over, and back up to cut out a square of the container. When the container is placed upside down in the enclosure, this cutout section will form the door into and out of the container. Again, be sure it's wide enough to allow your snake to crawl in and out easily.

Some snakes will push their hide boxes around in their cages, positioning them along the heating gradient so the hiding place is in the most comfortable temperature zone. If you have a large enough enclosure, you can place a hiding place at each end of the cage, one at the warm end and one at the cooler end.

Some reptile enclosures include built-in hiding places in which snakes can curl up to feel secure. What's neat about these, too, is that the caves in which the snake can hide are built against the glass of the terrarium wall, which means you can see the snake while it's in the hiding place.

branches that snakes can crawl on, a snake cage doesn't generally need to contain too many other objects. Because of this, the cages are pretty easy to set up and maintain. Some hobbyists use artificial plants, too, but these can be damaged by heavy snakes.

Driftwood and grapewood branches are often for sale at pet and reptile stores as well as at reptile expos. When you put these in a snake enclosure, be sure they're firmly in place and that they can't fall down or be moved around by the snake. Some keepers will screw branches to the sides of the enclosure, or wedge them into place, especially if the branches are high up in the cage. This is most commonly done in homemade enclosures built of wood or melamine (a plastic-coated wood product), so the branches can be attached to the walls (something that's harder to do with glass).

Lighting and Heating

When you visit a pet store, you'll see all kinds of lighting and heating equipment for reptiles. You need to know what kinds your snake will need to stay healthy.

Proper Lighting

Some reptiles, especially basking turtles and lizards, need

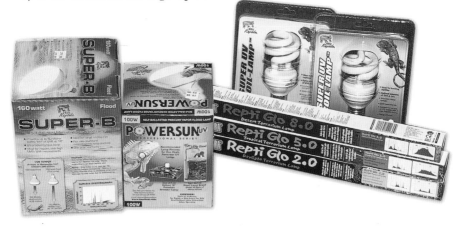

Although snakes receive proper nutrition from the prey they eat, many keepers still provide ultraviolet lighting to ensure good health.

A good reptile or pet store will have a variety of products available to help you take proper care of your snakes.

ultraviolet (UV) lighting to stay healthy. Snakes, however, don't really need it. The reason the other reptiles do is because ultraviolet lighting provides vitamins and minerals the animals don't usually get from the foods they eat in captivity. Snakes, though, get all the nutrition they need from their prey; the bones of the rodents they eat even provide the snakes with necessary calcium.

Of course, providing UV lighting won't hurt a snake, and some keepers will use this type of lighting (in the form of fluorescent tubes) anyway. Other keepers use standard incandescent or fluorescent light fixtures to illuminate their snake enclosures.

Gradient Heating

As discussed earlier, snakes, like all reptiles, are cold-blooded animals, so they depend on outside temperatures to regulate their body heat. If it's cold in the enclosure, a snake's body temperature goes down, and if it's hot, the body temperature goes up. Most pet snakes prefer temperatures warmer than room temperature and need them to digest food.

You don't, however, want the entire cage to be the same temperature. You want a cage with a **heat gradient**, or **thermal gradient**. (This is a common part of all reptile housing.) That means one end of your snake's cage is cooler than the other. This allows the animal inside to choose the area in the cage that's most comfortable for it.

Heating in a snake enclosure can be provided by heat lamps, heat tape, undertank heaters, infrared heating elements, and other heating devices. All of these can be purchased at stores that sell reptile supplies. Read the

Placing heat mats, tape, lights, and other heating elements at one end of the enclosure will allow your snake to thermoregulate.

I need warm temperatures to digest my food.

directions on the packaging to be sure you are using the devices correctly. Thermostats are often included, so you can set the temperature on the heating element to make certain that the enclosure doesn't get too hot (or remain too cold) for your snake.

To create a heat gradient, all you need to do is concentrate any heating you're providing on one end of the cage. Place the heat lamp at that end, or put the undertank heater there. If your snake wants to warm up, it will move toward the warm side of the cage. If it wants to cool down, it will move toward the other side. When the animal moves around based on the temperature at which it feels most comfy, it is **thermoregulating**.

Use a thermometer to keep track of the temperature inside your snake enclosure, too.

California kingsnake

Having one at both ends of the enclosure is a good idea.

If you use a heating device that is actually in the cage with the snake, you need to be sure the snake can't come into direct contact with it. If it can, the snake may be burned (read more about this in chapter 8). Some heating elements come with wire attachments to keep snakes away from them. If yours doesn't, you can cover the device with screening. Again, read the instructions that come with the heater before setting it up, and ask pet store employees or reptile-knowledgeable people for help if you're unsure about safety issues.

Creating a Habitat Background

Enclosures that look like a little piece of nature are particularly eye catching. If you want to get really creative, you could paint a background to attach to your snake's enclosure. This can look nice if you have a glass cage that you can see through to the back. Here's what you'll need:

☑ Poster board to paint your background on. You could also use anything that you would be able to attach to the back wall of your snake's enclosure (thin wood, cardboard, butcher's paper, and so on).

☑ Paint and markers or colored pencils. Use a water-based paint. Acrylic paints are available in many different colors and can be washed off with water; you can find them in craft and art stores. Watercolors can look really nice, too, either alone or with acrylics. Use colored pencils or markers—whatever you like to use to create art!

☑ Paintbrushes of various sizes

☑ Yardstick

☑ Scissors

☑ Tape

Use the yardstick to measure the back wall of the enclosure, and use scissors to cut your paper to fit the wall. Then paint or draw whatever you like on your background. You could try to make your painting look like the area where your species of snake lives. If you're keeping a California

This fancy, three-part setup has its own "painted desert" background. Use it as an inspiration for your artistic creation!

mountain kingsnake or a rosy boa, for instance, you could paint a desert landscape. If you're keeping a ball python, you could paint a tropical-looking background.

Of course, you can paint whatever you want, but natural-looking habitat backgrounds usually have the nicest appearance. Get creative.

Once you're finished and the paint has dried, use the tape to attach your masterpiece to the back of your snake's enclosure. Sit back, and enjoy your artistic efforts!

CHAPTER 5

Snake Food

T his isn't going to be a very long chapter because all the snakes I recommend for beginners eat mice and rats. (I'll be talking about those great beginner snakes in the next chapter.) The western hognose snake (see page 74) does eat toads in the wild, but captive-bred hognoses will usually eat mice. If you get one that doesn't gobble down its mouse dinner, it is probably a wild-caught hognose. To get it to eat, you may have to scent the mouse with a toad (this means you rub the toad against the mouse to get the toad scent on the mouse). All the other snakes I recommend should readily eat rodents.

Corn snake

Before you buy a snake, be sure you can provide it with the right type of food. The owner of this snake might need a ready supply of toads.

Live or Not?

Although the snake menu may be a bit limited, there is one important question you need to consider in regard to feeding your snakes: Do you feed it live food or not?

Frozen Dinner

Did you know that you can buy frozen rodents to feed your snakes? There are some benefits to offering frozen-then-thawed mice and rats to your pets. One benefit is that it's safer for your snake. After all, a live rodent can bite your snake. Another benefit is that the freezing process can kill any potentially harmful parasites that may be in or on the rodent and could affect your snake.

Some people are squeamish about feeding live rodents to their snakes. Using frozen rodents doesn't seem quite as "icky" to them.

Storing frozen rodents is also easier and less smelly than keeping a supply of live mice and rats in the house and can save you trips to the pet store to buy them. Of course, fellow family members may not love the idea of having frozen rodents next to the frozen vegetables and popsicles in the freezer.

Dinner on the Run

If you offer a live rodent to your snake, about all you have to do is drop the mouse or rat into the enclosure. A hungry snake will usually waste no time in finding its dinner. If the snake does not eat the rodent right away, remove the rodent and try some other time. *Never*

Clean Rodents Only

When you are purchasing live rodents to feed your snakes, take note of how clean the rodents' cages are. If they are filthy, the rodents may not be well. Because you want to feed only healthy rodents to your snakes, think twice about buying feeder mice or rats that look unwell. If you feed a sick rodent to your snake, your pet may get sick, too.

This young speckled kingsnake is gobbling a pinky mouse. The mouse is called a pinky because it has yet to grow hair.

Rodents such as mice and rats are very popular prey items for pet snakes. This Texas rat snake has constricted a mouse and is about to swallow it.

Feeding Frequency

Snakes generally need to be fed only a couple of times a week. If you feed them smaller prey items, however, you may need to feed them more often. Big snakes that can eat big meals sometimes can go a long time between feeding. Huge constrictors have been known to go up to a year without eating! Of course, it is not recommended that keepers wait that long to feed their pets!

leave a live rodent in the snake enclosure unsupervised, especially overnight. If you do, the rodent could bite your snake and cause serious injury.

If someone else is around at feeding time, don't try to make that person watch you feed your snake unless he or she wants to. Some people do get a thrill when watching a snake hunt and kill its prey, which is a natural process. But others don't like seeing it. Always respect their feelings, just as you would want yours respected. Don't try to make someone watch something he or she doesn't want to see.

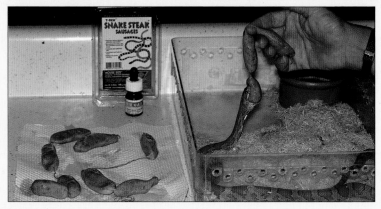

Feeding frozen and thawed rodents isn't the only way to avoid feeding live prey to snakes. There are also snake sausages, which are made of ground-up meat and formed into sausage-like links. Just be careful if you ever happen to have any out during a BBQ, as they could easily be mistaken for people food!

Tease-Feeding and Force-Feeding

Sometimes snakes won't eat. This can happen for different reasons, such as the snake is not well or it is scared. And sometimes a snake just won't eat, for no reason you can determine.

If a snake refuses to eat, there are some steps you can take. The first is to try again later. If the snake continues to refuse food, and you've been offering thawed frozen items, you can try **tease-feeding** the snake.

Tease-feeding is when you jiggle the prey item in front of your snake so it looks like it's alive. This can be done using a pair of long forceps (they look kind of like long skinny tweezers).

If a snake still won't eat, it may need to be force-fed. Beginners should not attempt force-feeding on their own. Ask someone who knows how to do this task to handle it for you.

Feeding prekilled prey to snakes can be safer because live prey can injure snakes. Tongs come in handy for this, especially if the snake being fed is a venomous one!

Force-feeding requires the snake's mouth to be carefully pried open and the food placed into it. The food item is gently inserted until the snake begins swallowing on its own. Again, a beginner should not attempt this. If the procedure goes well, the snake will swallow the food item. If it doesn't go well, the snake may **regurgitate** (throw up) the item.

That's about all you need to know about snake food. Now let's look at some snakes that make the best beginner pets.

The Right Size

Feeder mice and rats are sold in different sizes, from newborn **pinkies** (called that because of their hairless pink skin) and **fuzzies** (young rodents that are starting to grow hair) up to adults. Offer the size that's appropriate for your snake. A good way to do this is to not offer a prey item that is larger than the snake is at its widest point.

CHAPTER 6

Great Beginner Snakes

Before you visit a pet store or a reptile expo and see a bunch of cool-looking snakes, you should learn about them. Otherwise, you could end up with the wrong snake for you. Beginners, especially, should choose carefully because some of those small snakes you see very likely won't stay small for long. They could get really big!

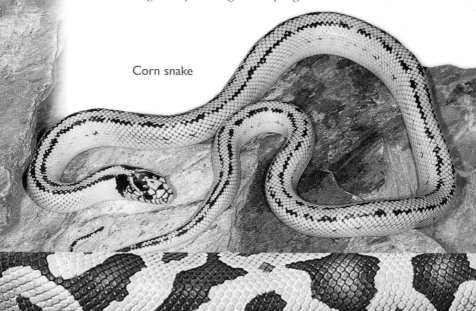

Corn snake

In this chapter, we'll look at snakes that beginners should have no problem keeping. Generally, the species mentioned here are considered good starter snakes. This means they don't get too huge, they have no hard-to-meet considerations in regard to their care, and they generally have good manners. Remember, though, all animals are individuals. So even a snake species with a reputation for being nice may include a few specimens that will bite, be intolerant of handling, or have other negative reactions. But again, the snakes we talk about below are generally considered excellent beginner species.

The corn snake is a great first snake for beginners.

Basic care tips are provided in this chapter; for additional housing and feeding information, see chapters 4 and 5.

Corn Snake

No snake says "I'm the best beginner snake" quite as well as the corn snake (*Elaphe guttata*) does. Don't think the corn snake gets this name because it eats corn—it eats rodents such as mice and rats. There are a cou- ple stories about why it's called corn snake. One is that it can be found in cornfields, and the other is that the colors and pattern of the belly scales on a normal corn snake resemble maize (Indian corn). I personally think

A Snake's Other Name

All living things, including snakes, are known by common names (such as corn snake) and scientific names (in the case of the corn snake, *Elaphe guttata*). Taxonomy is the science used to place animals and plants into categories. Taxonomy, with its use of scientific names, is a very complicated subject, but I'll give you the basics.

The two words that make up an animal's Latin name are the *genus* (first word) and *species* (second word). For the corn snake, the word *Elaphe* is the genus name and *guttata* is the species name. There can be other species within a genus, too. For instance, the black rat snake belongs to the same genus as the corn snake does. Its Latin name is *Elaphe obsoleta*.

the second reason is the most interesting, but I don't think anyone knows for sure which might be the right one. And maybe neither explanation is.

Wild corn snakes have a large range: from northern New Jersey down into and throughout the southeastern United States and west into Kentucky and Missouri. The average length of a corn snake is about 4 feet (1.2 m). The "normal" corn snake (in other words, one that exhibits the standard coloration and that is not a color mutation) is a very pretty snake, with an orange yellow body and darker orange red blotches outlined

in black. This is far from the only type of corn snake available as a pet. Over the years, by breeding different types of corn snakes together, breeders have created many interesting and pretty corn snake color varieties, such as ghosts, sunglows, blood-reds, and creamsicles, to name just a few. Mutations such as these cost more than normal corn snakes do. They also don't appear in the wild. If they did, they would probably be killed by predators because those unique colors would make the snakes stand out. Normal-colored animals are colored the way they are to **camouflage**

These are all corn snakes. Because of captive-breeding, corn (and other) snakes are available in many different colors. This keeps the hobby interesting!

them (meaning help them blend in with their surroundings to hide from predators).

Pet corn snakes can be kept in 20-gallon (76-liter [L]) aquariums or reptile enclosures of the same size. Reptile carpet, newspaper, or orchid bark can be used as a substrate. Avoid dusty substrates, such as pine shavings. Avoid cedar, too, as it contains oils that can be toxic to snakes. As with any snake, be sure the top of the enclosure is very secure because snakes are excellent escape artists.

A Corn Snake's Other Name

Corn snakes are also known as red rat snakes. There are many other types of rat snakes (*Elaphe*), including yellow rats, Everglades rats, and gray rats. Generally, rat snakes reach about 4 feet (1.2 m) in length. Most of them are considered gentle, although some (such as yellow rat snakes) can be jumpier than others.

There should be a heat gradient in the cage. As we talked about in chapter 4, in the "Gradient Heating" section, this means one end of the enclosure should be warmer than the other. The hot end of a corn snake's cage should be in the low to mid 80s F (high 20s to low 30s C).

Provide at least one hiding spot, such as a piece of bark or a hide box, into which the snake can slither to feel secure. Two hiding spots can be even better, with one at the warm end of the cage and the other at the cooler end. Hiding places are very important for pet snakes to feel secure, so don't forget to provide at least one. Provide also a small water bowl, one that would be hard to tip over. Change the water at least once a day or sooner, if necessary.

As mentioned, corn snakes, which are **constrictors**, eat mice and rats. Feeding your corn snake an appropriate-size (no bigger than the snake is at its widest point) mouse or small rat once a week is sufficient.

The Mechanics of Constricting

Many big and small snakes—including corn snakes, kingsnakes, and pythons—constrict their prey and so are called constrictors. When a snake coils around prey such as a mouse, it may look like the snake is crushing the rodent to death and breaking its bones. But that's not what the snake is doing. It is subduing the mouse by suffocation. The snake patiently holds the mouse in its coils, and each time the mouse breathes out, the snake tightens its coils a little more. Eventually, this makes it impossible for the mouse to breathe in, the mouse suffocates, and down the hatch it goes, usually headfirst.

The California kingsnake is a famously easygoing snake that is a favorite with snake keepers. Like most snakes, it will eat rodents.

California Kingsnake

Kingsnakes, in general, are famous for being gentle, friendly snakes. There are many different types, which range across the United States. The California kingsnake (*Lampropeltis getula californiae*), also known as the Cal king, is the one that many people consider the best beginner kingsnake pet.

As with corn snakes, the captive-breeding efforts with kingsnakes have resulted in different color and pattern types of California kingsnakes. These include, among others, banana, lavender, snow, and desert kings. The normal type, however, is banded in white and black, brown and white, or brown and yellow. In nature, these kingsnakes occur in California, of course, but also can be found in Arizona, Nevada, Utah, and Baja California.

Adult Cal kings average about 4 feet (1.2 m) in length, so an enclosure similar in size to a 20-gallon (76-L) aquarium is fine for them. Other basic care requirements in regard to substrate, temperature, and other aspects are the same as those given for corn snakes. Kingsnakes are constrictors, and pet snakes will accept mice and rats.

One fact you need to keep in mind about California kingsnakes: although they eat mice and rats, they're also cannibals and will eat other snakes. Wild Cal kings will even eat rattlesnakes! A Cal king can't be kept with another snake because it will eat the other snake. So remember this important point if you want a Cal king for a pet—keep it by itself.

Ball Python

For the most part, pythons are not recommended for beginner snake hobbyists. This group of snakes

includes the biggest snake in the word, the reticulated python. The Burmese python, too, which is commonly sold as a pet, gets huge and really, really heavy.

An exception to the pythons-are-huge rule is the ball python (*Python regius*), also known as the royal python. Adult ball pythons average 3 to 4 feet (1 to 1.2 m) in length. The ball python is from Africa, where the normal-colored ball python is black with a yellowish tan pattern. Once again, however, we have

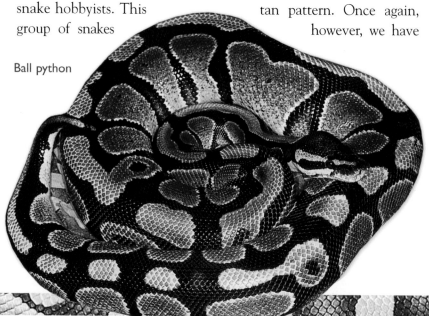

Ball python

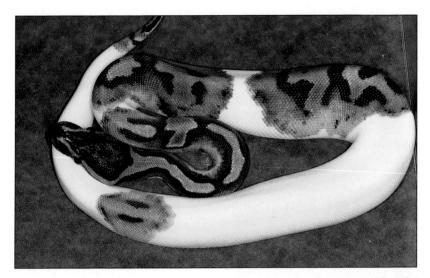

The "normal" type of ball python is quite affordable. There are many beautiful mutations, though—such as this "piebald" ball—and they can cost lots of money!

snake breeders to thank for producing a huge assortment of designer ball python color and pattern mutations that are now available for sale. Many of these are very expensive, especially when they first arrive on the reptile-keeping scene. As they become more common, the prices usually come down somewhat. Some ball python morphs (mutations) are very beautiful, including the spider, clown, and piebald balls.

Young ball pythons can be housed easily in enclosures that are the same size as those recommended for the two pet snakes discussed earlier, but because these snakes have bodies that are thicker than the other species mentioned here, a 55-gallon (208-L) aquarium is better for adult balls. A cage temperature in the high 70s to low 80s F (mid- to high 20s C) is OK, with a hot spot in the high 80s to low 90s F (low 30s C). Ball pythons, more than corn snakes and kingsnakes, require some humidity, so cages with sliding-glass fronts work well for them as opposed to aquariums with screen tops. (The screen makes it hard to maintain humidity levels.) A proper humidity level would be about 50 percent, which can be provided by occasional light misting with a water bottle or by keeping a lidded plastic container containing moist sphagnum moss in the cage. Cut a hole in the lid that is large enough to allow the python to enter and exit easily. This area can provide the snake

with both a moist spot and a hiding place. The substrate you use can affect humidity, too. Orchid bark and cypress mulch help maintain humidity levels.

Feed pet ball pythons a rat once a week. Young wild-caught ball pythons have a reputation for being difficult feeders, and this reputation has unfairly been passed on to all ball pythons. Captive-bred snakes, though, are not known for exhibiting this behavior. If their keepers are patient and persistent, even reluctant wild snakes can eventually be coaxed into accepting food. Just keep offering food until it is taken.

How the Ball Python Got Its Name

While defending themselves, many snakes will hiss, puff up, or try to slither away to safety. The ball python, though, has an unusual defensive maneuver. A frightened ball python will tuck its head into its coils and wrap its body around it, forming a ball that protects the snake's head. Hence the name ball python.

Western Hognose Snake

The hognose snakes (*Heterodon*), although generally more expensive than corn and kingsnakes, are very interest-

This hognose snake is playing dead.

ing, attractive snakes that are famous for a unique defense behavior. When frightened, a hognose snake will first do the usual things a snake that's threatened will do: hiss and strike. If that doesn't work, a hognose snake will flip itself onto its back, stick its tongue out, and pretend to be dead! It can be a very convincing display, and the hognose does it in the hope that a predator that wants to eat it will buzz off and go looking for live prey instead. Once a hognose is on its back, it will stay that way until it's sure the threat is gone. If you flip it onto its belly, it will flip itself right back over. A new pet hognose may do this occasionally, but as it gets used to its home, the playing-dead act will probably stop.

Hognoses can also inflate a hood, similar to a cobra's famous defense behavior, in an attempt to scare away an animal or person that it perceives as a threat. The hood is meant to make the snakes look bigger and more threatening.

Hognose snakes get their common name because their snouts are upturned, giving them a piglike appearance. The upturned snout helps the hognose when it's burrowing into soil, which it does while looking for food.

Of the various hognoses, the western (*Heterodon nasicus*) is the one most often suggested as a beginner pet. Wild western

Hognose snakes may hiss and puff up if they're scared.

A frightened hognose spreads its hood the way more dangerous cobras do.

hognoses are found in the U.S. Midwest. Adults are fairly small, typically reaching a length of about 2 feet (61 cm) or a bit longer. They have thick bodies that are tan or cream in color, with brown spots covering the body. In addition to the upturned snout, hognoses have another interesting physical feature that the other snakes in this chapter lack: keeled scales. Each scale along a hognose's back has a **keel**, or a raised ridge, along the center. This gives the hognoses a somewhat bumpy

Mildly Venomous

Hognose snakes, including the western hognose, are rear-fanged snakes that are mildly venomous but not to a level considered dangerous to people (unless a person is allergic to their venom). For one thing, the fangs that deliver the venom are far back in the snake's mouth, where your finger would be unlikely to encounter them. Besides that, the venom is not very strong: it's used mostly to kill toads, the primary food of wild hognoses. The fangs of a hognose are also used to puncture and deflate toads. Toads inflate themselves with air in self-defense, so the hognose has to deflate a puffed-up toad before it can swallow this particular prey.

Even though the hognose snake venom is not considered very dangerous, people may have reactions to it. If you have a reaction, such as painful irritation or swelling, a visit to the doctor is definitely in order.

appearance, as opposed to the smooth look of other snakes.

Pet western hognoses can be kept in enclosures such as those mentioned for the other snakes in this chapter, but because they're smaller than the other snakes, they could be kept in a cage as small as a 10-gallon (38-L) aquarium. (A 20-gallon (76-L) would be better, however). Although wild hognoses eat toads, birds, and other animals, a pet hognose will usually accept rodents, especially if the snake is a captive-bred specimen (another argument for buying captive-bred animals). Cage temperature should be in the mid-70s to low 80s F (mid- to high 20s C), with a hot end of 85°F (30°C). A paper substrate or reptile carpet can work for them, but providing aspen shavings or reptile sand will allow the hognose to spend time burrowing. Be sure the substrate is a product that's safe for the snake to eat and digest, in case it accidentally swallows some.

Now you know some snakes that you could keep fairly easily and that would make good pets for first-time snake keepers. In the next chapter, we'll take a quick look at a few other snakes that are not recommended for beginner hobbyists, including really big species and venomous ones. Just because they're not recommended as pets for you doesn't

Have you hugged your hognose today?

Western hognose snake

mean you shouldn't know about them. As you'll see, they're worth knowing about!

A Good Beginner Boa

Boa constrictors can get quite large, and I would not recommend them for novice snake keepers. However, there is a snake that's in the boa family that I would recommend for beginners: the rosy boa (*Lichanura trivirgata*). It is one of only two boas found in the United States (the other is the rubber boa). Rosies are known for being quite tame, and they seldom bite. (Of course, this doesn't mean that this snake *never* bites—but rosies have small mouths.) Pet rosy boas will eat mice.

The rosy boa is a smallish snake (adults don't usually get much bigger than 3 feet, or 1 m, in length) that can be housed comfortably in a 20-gallon (76-L) aquarium or other enclosure of similar size. They like to burrow, so reptile sand (available in pet stores) or play sand (available in toy stores and do-it-yourself centers) can be used as a substrate, as can small aspen chips or even newspaper, though newspaper wouldn't allow burrowing. The enclosure should have good ventilation and low humidity, both of which can be provided by a screen top. The average temperature for a rosy boa enclosure can be from the mid-70s F (mid-

The rosy boa is one of only two boa species (the other is the rubber boa) found in the United States. "Rosies" are usually quite tame in captivity.

The Children's Python

Although the ball python is usually considered the best python for snake-keeping newbies, the Children's python (*Antaresia childreni*) is another small python that is quite gentle and can be a good pet. It comes from Australia (although it is being bred in captivity now), and adults usually reach between 2 to 3 feet (76 to 91 cm) in length. This python is sometimes considered slightly snappy, but not to a huge degree, and it's not known for frequent biting behavior. It's an attractive snake, with reddish brown spots on a light tan body. In the wild, it eats lizards, birds, and rodents, but pets will usually do OK on rodents only.

The Children's python does not get its common name because it's considered a good pet for children. It's named after the man who described it back when it was first discovered: John George Children, who was a curator at the British Museum.

20s C) in the cooler end of the cage to the mid-80s (high 20s to low 30s C) at the warm end. As with all pet snakes, provide a hiding place.

The common name of rosy boa comes from the snake's color, which is grayish pink, with three reddish stripes running the length of the body. The head, which is covered with many very small scales, is not as distinct from the body as the heads of other snakes are; the rosy boa's head sort of blends into its body. The tail is fairly short and rounded.

Wild rosy boas can be found in Southern California and western Arizona, where they are most active at dusk. Keep this in mind if you want a rosy for a pet: you may not see it moving about much in the daytime.

Rosy boa constrictors sometimes exhibit the same balling-up defense behavior that ball pythons are famous for.

CHAPTER 7

Other Amazing Snakes

When you watch television shows about reptiles, they often feature giant constrictors such as anacondas and reticulated pythons, or venomous snakes such as rattlesnakes and cobras. One reason is that these snakes have a very commanding presence. When you see a huge python, you might gasp in awe (or, in the case of certain people, fright), and watching a cobra flare its hood and hiss is certainly impressive. Some cobras can even spit venom! Needless to say, I can't recommend these types of snakes as pets for someone just getting started in the wonderful world of snake keeping.

King cobra

In addition, big species need larger cages. (For certain really big snakes, you might eventually need to provide each one with a room of its own in your house rather than keep it in a typical snake enclosure.) You also have to be skilled in handling and caring for them. Some of these snakes, especially venomous ones such as cobras, are outright dangerous. So, of course, beginners should not even think about keeping them.

Still, a lot of these snakes are fascinating animals in their own right and deserve mention in this book. Let's take a look at some of the really impressive types.

Boa Constrictor

The boa constrictor (*Boa constrictor*) is the boa people most commonly keep as pets. Wild boa constrictors come from Central and South America. Their colors and patterns can vary depending on where in Central and South America they live. The most popular pet boa constrictors have a gray to

The red-tailed boa is popular, but it gets pretty big.

creamy tan background color, with blotches of maroon along the entire length of the body, all the way down to the tail. This is how the popular red-tailed boa constrictors got their common name. On some, the red coloration is particularly bright and pretty; on others, it's darker.

Depending on the type, adult boa constrictors can grow to about 12 feet (3.7 m) in length; other types average about 7 feet (2 m). Just as with the beginner snakes mentioned in the previous chapter, boa breeders have bred some cool color morphs of boa constrictors,

Although it can get fairly large, the red-tailed boa constrictor is usually gentle and is often the first boa constrictor that people keep.

including salmon boas (they have a pinkish hue) and albinos with red eyes.

Boa constrictors are usually calm snakes. (Keep in mind, however, that even snakes known for being gentle can sometimes get a bit grumpy.) Therefore, boa constrictors are often recommended as good snakes for people who are just beginning to keep larger snakes.

Mama Python

Boas give birth to live young; pythons lay eggs. After laying a **clutch** (which means a group of eggs), the female python will wrap herself around the eggs to keep them warm and incubate them. Professional python breeders will typically remove  the eggs from the female to incubate them in an incubator, which is a device that keeps the eggs warm and at the proper level of humidity so they will hatch normally.

Garter Snakes

Garter snakes (genus *Thamnophis*) are quite common in a number of areas of the United States, and they are often the first snakes many people encounter in nature. There are various types of garter snakes, and some are very pretty. Probably the most beautiful is the San Francisco garter snake (*Thamnophis sirtalis tetrataenia*, pictured above), which is, unfortunately, an endangered species that is hard to find.

Although garter snakes are very common and introduce many people to the world of snakes and snake keeping, I don't usually recommend them as pets for beginners. That's why they're mentioned in this chapter rather than in the previous chapter. The snakes in chapter 6 are known for being mellow snakes that are good for novice snake hobbyists. Garter snakes, by contrast, can be skittish and slow to tame down. They can be feisty and often nervous in captivity. So while some may relax and be good pets, I still think the snakes in the previous chapter are better beginner snakes than garters are.

Burmese Python

Here's a real biggie. One particularly large Burmese python (*Python molurus bivittatus*) was said to be 27 feet (8.2 m) long and weigh 403 pounds (183 kg)! Of course, even that snake started out small, just like the cute baby Burmese pythons for sale in your local reptile store or at an expo. But those babies, given the proper care, will grow and grow. Remember this if you ever think you want to own one.

The normal color for a Burmese python is a tannish

Albino Burmese python

Don't buy me if you can't care for me.

cream color with brown blotches all over its body. These snakes are bred regularly in captivity. Wild Burmese pythons live in Southeast Asia, including Myanmar, once called Burma (and the reason for the snake's common name).

Albino Burmese pythons are plentiful, and these snakes are beautiful. On an albino, the cream color of the normal Burmese is white and the brown patches are bright yellow. So they're big yellow and white snakes with red eyes. Gorgeous!

Unfortunately, pet Burmese pythons suffer a sad consequence of their size. Ignorant would-be snake hobbyists who did not read about the snake before they bought one find themselves with a rapidly growing—and growing and growing—snake on their hands.

Beginners should not buy Burmese pythons. These snakes, while they make good pets for people who can house them properly, get huge!

The Egg Eaters

In this book, you've already read about snakes that eat rodents, toads, birds, and other animals. As their name indicates, the egg eaters of Africa eat eggs. Egg-eating snakes of the genus *Dasypeltis* will swallow an egg, and muscles in the throat will constrict and crush the egg. The gooey raw egg is swallowed, and the crushed shell is spit out.

Some of these snakes are kept in captivity by advanced hobbyists, who will often feed them quail eggs.

When the Burmese outgrows the original cage, the owner decides to find a new home for it. He or she may ask pet stores and maybe even zoos whether they will take the snake, but finding a new home for a large Burmese python can be difficult. So the owner either drops the snake at an animal shelter or—the worst decision ever—sets the snake "free" into the wild.

At the time I'm writing this book, there are reports of ex-pet Burmese pythons popping up in Everglades National Park in Florida. This is not good, as the snakes' being there defies the natural order of nature, and they can have bad effects on the animals that are supposed to live there (by eating them,

for instance). *Never* release an unwanted pet into the wild!

Overall, for advanced keepers who are able to care for such a large snake, the Burmese python is usually a friendly pet. Young Burmese pythons will eat the usual menu of rats. However, as these snakes attain their large sizes, they will eventually eat rabbits and other larger mammals.

Reticulated Python

Here is another huge snake. As a matter of fact, according to some sources, the reticulated python (*Python reticulatus*) is the largest snake in the world. Adult retics can reach lengths of more than 30 feet (9 m).

One of the largest snakes in the world, the beautiful reticulated python, can grow to more than 30 feet in length!

They're long, but not as thick as other large snakes, such as Burmese pythons, are. Wild retics live in Southeast Asia (including Malaysia, Myanmar, and Indochina) and Indonesia. They prefer to live near water within their jungle habitat.

These snakes are, in my opinion, one of the most beautiful species. They can vary in color but most often have a background color of tan, with orange and black markings. They have striking (no pun intended) orange eyes, too. The reticulated python gets its common name because of the geometric pattern it exhibits.

Unfortunately, the beauty of this species has a sad side effect: wild specimens are regularly killed for their skins, which are made into belts, purses, shoes, and other fashion accessories.

Reticulated pythons have a reputation for being feisty in captivity, but this is most likely based on the behavior of wild-caught snakes. Still, they have large fangs, and caution is warranted when keeping them. Like any large snake, a retic requires lots of space. This is most definitely a snake that should be kept only by advanced snake keepers, not by beginners.

Anaconda

The runner-up in the competition for the title of World's Largest Snake, the anaconda lives in swampy habitat throughout South America. Of the four species of anaconda, the green anaconda (*Eunectes murinus*) is the best known.

Another biggie is the anaconda—it can grow to 25 feet.

Adults can reach about 25 feet (7.6 m) in length. These are thick, heavy-bodied snakes, light olive in color with dark spots. They spend a lot of time in the water and are excellent swimmers. Like many of the other snakes already discussed, big and small, the anaconda, too, is a constrictor that eats warm-blooded mammals.

Although anacondas can get very large, they *cannot* get as big as the one in the movie *Anaconda*. That one was not based much on reality. Anacondas—real and imagined—seem to be a favored snake on the big screen and on TV. For years, on nature programs, it seemed that every so often someone would end up wrestling an anaconda in the water. I think even Tarzan may have gotten into the act a few times. All of this is kind of funny when you consider that all a snake usually wants to do is get away and hide from people. Anacondas are very powerful, though—I sure wouldn't want to fight one underwater!

Green Tree Python

This is a very pretty python, and it's common to see this snake for sale at reptile expos. An adult green tree python

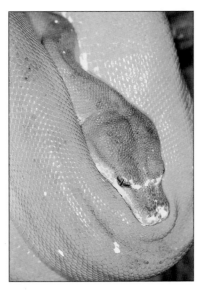

Some green tree pythons are more bluish in color.

Chondropython) can reach lengths of about 6 feet (1.8 m). Pets are generally fed rats. Wild-caught green tree pythons have a reputation for being "bitey," but captive-bred snakes are known to tame up in captivity. Still, they've got big python heads and big teeth inside those heads!

An interesting fact about the green tree python is that the babies look totally different from the adults. Baby chondros hatch from their eggs as bright yellow, dark red, or chocolate brown snakes. As they grow older, the green coloration takes over. This is called an **ontogenetic color change**. The green tree python is a popular snake with breeders, who work to create new color morphs.

(*Morelia viridis*) is usually a green or (less common) bluish snake that may exhibit flecks of blue, white, or yellow coloration on its body. Adult chondros (called that because their old genus name was

Green tree python, yellow hatchling

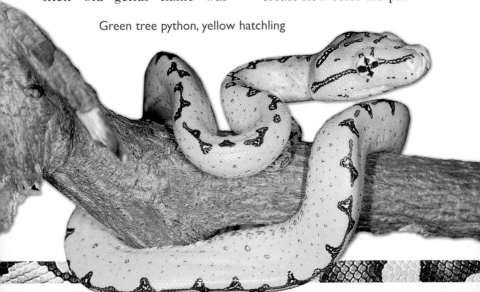

Carpet Python

Another beautiful python, the carpet python (*Morelia spilota*), is from Australia. Although some can grow larger, adults are usually between 6 and 7 feet (between 1.8 and 2 m) in length. The coloration is most often yellow with brown blotches and reticulations.

This is another python often recommended as a good beginner species for people starting out with their first larger snakes. Carpet pythons are usually quite calm as adults and are not known to be grumpy and skittish

The carpet python is a real looker and makes a good pet.

(although young snakes might be a little nippy). So after you have some snake-keeping experience with the snakes mentioned in chapter 6, this is one you might want to consider giving a try someday.

Tentacled Snake

This very unusual snake lives in Asia. The tentacled snake (*Erpeton tentaculatum*) is an aquatic snake that gets its name because of the two projections (the "tentacles") that poke out from its snout. Why does the snake have these tentacles? No one knows for sure, but it's thought that they help the snake find the small fish it waits to ambush.

The tentacled snake is a small (about 20 inches [51 cm]) reddish brown snake with keeled scales, so if you were to feel one, its body would feel rough and kind of "jaggedy." This is another rear-fanged species (like the hognose snake mentioned in chapter 6), so it is mildly venomous but not particularly dangerous to humans. Although the tentacled snake lives in the water, it does have to surface to breathe air. It can stay underwater for about a half hour between breaths.

Rhinoceros Viper

Here's another snake with an interesting facial feature. Can you guess why the rhinoceros viper (*Bitis nasicornis*) is called that? As you may know, a rhinoceros is a big animal that has horns on its head. Well, so does the rhino viper: it has "horns" that stick up from its snout.

The venomous rhino viper lives in Africa and usually grows to about 4 feet (1.2 m) in length. It's one of the puff adders, a group of venomous snakes that can puff themselves up with air as a defensive maneuver. Doing this makes the snake look bigger, which can scare off predators. The rhino viper is a very pretty snake that exhibits a complicated pattern of blue, black, gray, orange, and other colors.

Rattlesnakes

I'm willing to bet you're at least a little familiar with rattlesnakes and know that they are so named because of the rattles they have on the ends of their tails, which they will vibrate as a warning.

See those horns on this rhinoceros viper's snout? It's easy to see how this venomous snake comes by its common name.

Did you know there are snakes that swim in the ocean? These are the sea snakes, and being relatives of the cobras, they are very venomous, although their teeth are quite small. While sea snakes swim and feed

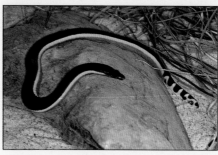

on fish in the ocean, some of them do emerge from the water, taking refuge in rock crevices and crawling along land. Some lay eggs on land, too, while others have babies in the water. All sea snakes breathe air, so they have to come to the surface when swimming in the ocean.

The heads of sea snakes are about the same thickness as their bodies, and they have paddle-shaped tails that aid them in swimming. Most can be found swimming along the coasts of Asia and Australia. One, the yellow-bellied sea snake (*Pelamis platurus*), is **pelagic**, which means it can be found swimming in the open ocean far from shore.

There are many different types of rattlesnakes. The biggest is the eastern diamondback (*Crotalus adamanteus*), which can grow to 8 feet (2.4 m), although 5 to 6 feet (1.5 to 1.8 m) is the most common length. It is the largest venomous snake in North America, and it gets its name from the diamond pattern found along its back. It's a pretty rattler, with a tan or gray background color and brownish diamonds outlined in yellow or cream. It lives throughout Florida as well as in coastal lowlands from southeastern North Carolina to eastern Louisiana. Wild eastern diamondbacks will frequently live in gopher tortoise burrows.

The eastern diamondback has a western counterpart in the western diamondback rat-

This is a western diamondback rattlesnake. Rattlesnakes are among the best-known types of venomous snakes. If you leave them alone, they'll leave you alone.

tlesnake (*C. atrox*), which is smaller—it can grow up to 6 feet (1.8 m) long, but 4 feet (1.2 m) is more likely—and browner than the eastern diamondback, and it lives in Arizona, Arkansas, California, Nevada, New Mexico, Oklahoma, and Texas.

Another interesting rattlesnake is the sidewinder (*C. cerastes*), which lives in desert habitat in Arizona, California, and Nevada. It's a small snake, reaching about 2 feet (61 cm) in length. Its coloration is a mix of brown, white, and black, and there is a small hornlike projection over each eye. This rattler gets its name from the way it slithers along in a sideways motion. If you watch one that's moving quickly over sand dunes, it can almost look like it's flying over them.

King Cobra

Cobra varieties abound, but I thought we'd stick with the king. As if its staring eyes and venomous properties are not intimidating enough, the king cobra (*Ophiophagus hannah*) is also a large snake that can reach more than 18 feet (5.5 m) in length. This, along with the fact that it can kill you, makes it a pretty tough customer in the snake realm! King cobras live in Southeast Asia (including Malaysia and the Philippines) as well as in China and India.

The king cobra exhibits the famous defensive behavior for which cobras are known. If threatened, it will lift part of its body up off the ground and spread its hood. Because it can grow to an impressive length, a king cobra can lift the front portion of its body off the

Snake Charming

Have you ever seen a snake charmer on TV? In India, a man—the snake charmer—will sit next to a woven basket and begin playing a flute. A cobra will then rise up out of the basket, weaving back and forth as if it's hypnotized by the music.

The thing is, the cobra can't really hear the music the way we would. It may sense some vibration because of it, but the reason the cobra sways back and forth is likely because it's following the motion of the flute as it's moved back and forth by the snake charmer.

Getting a cobra to rise up is no big deal—they do this naturally in defense. So a cobra that rises out of a snake charmer's basket is doing what comes naturally. Seeing a man holding a flute, which is being moved from side to side, the snake follows this movement, swaying from side to side. And there you have the scene: a snake that looks as if it's been charmed into swaying back and forth by the snake charmer's music.

The king cobra is an impressive snake. It can grow to 18 feet and can lift the front half of its body off the ground to stare you in the eye—plus, it's deadly.

ground, which means it could stare an adult human in the eye. That's kind of creepy when you think about it.

The hood-spreading behavior is accomplished when a cobra flattens the ribs at the upper area of its spine. When they are flattened, they spread out a flap of skin on the back of the cobra's head, thus fanning out the hood. This behavior is usually accompanied by loud hissing. If all this doesn't scare off whatever may be tormenting a cobra, the tormentor probably deserves to be bitten!

Although they may have some scary qualities, cobras are like any other snake in that they would prefer to avoid face-to-face confrontations with people and will make every effort to escape rather than attack someone.

OK, so now you know about some cool snakes. (And, once again, I'm not suggesting that you, a beginner snake keeper, should keep any of them. In fact, you shouldn't!) It's time to learn how to go about making sure the snake you do get stays healthy and how to spot potential health problems.

Here's Looking at You!

The green vine snake (*Ahaetulla nasuta*) lives in rain forests in Asia. Its slender green body allows it to blend in well with the trees and vegetation through which it slithers while looking for birds, lizards, and frogs.

The bright green coloration makes this an attractive snake. Another startling feature of the green vine snake is its eyes: the eyes of a green vine snake are quite big compared with those of other snakes, and it has horizontal pupils. This is definitely one snake that can give the impression that it's staring at you! You may see this snake for sale, but remember that it is another mildly venomous species that should not be kept by beginners. It can grow to 6 feet (1.8 m) or so in length, and it's pretty fast. It's also **arboreal**, meaning it lives among branches, leaves, and yes, vines. Its green coloration helps it blend in with this habitat, where it will wait to ambush birds and other small animals.

CHAPTER 8

Potential Health Problems

When you get a snake—or any pet, for that matter—it's up to you to take care of it properly. You need to learn about it so you know what it eats, the temperature it needs in its enclosure, and what kind of substrate it should be crawling around on. Knowing as much as you can about an animal before you take it home always provides the best chance that you and your pet will be together for many years to come.

Rhinoceros viper

Even if you have done your homework and think you have found out everything you can about how to properly take care of an animal, there is still a chance you could someday end up with a sick one. Sometimes an animal become ill through no fault of yours. For instance, it might be sick when you acquire it. (Chapter 3 provides hints about how to pick a healthy pet.) Yet, sad as it is to say, more often a snake becomes sick because of something its caretaker did wrong. It may not have been offered the right type of foods, or maybe it wasn't kept in the right kind of enclosure at the correct temperature, or perhaps warning signs of illness were ignored or not recognized.

If your snake ever gets sick, my primary piece of advice is to take it to a veterinarian (or "vet" for short). If possible, find a vet who specializes in reptiles. For a tip on how to do that, read the "Finding a Reptile Veterinarian" box.

In this chapter, we're going to look at some health problems that can affect snakes.

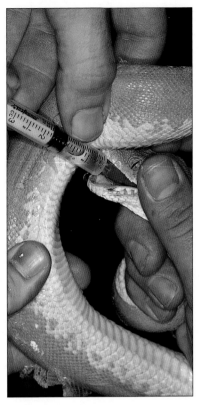

Medicating snakes can be tricky; let a vet do it.

This information is not meant to be an in-depth discussion of disease, and it is not meant to replace a visit to the veterinarian. It is presented to help you avoid certain conditions that could lead to your pet's becoming sick and to aid you in recognizing that something is wrong.

As I said above, I always recommend that you take your pet to a vet at the first sign of

Finding a Reptile Veterinarian

If you're not sure where to find a veterinarian who treats snakes, a good place to start, besides asking a local veterinarian, is the Web site for the Association of Reptilian and Amphibian Veterinarians (ARAV). This is a nonprofit international organization whose membership is composed of veterinarians who are particularly interested in, and knowledgeable about, reptiles. You can find the Web site at http://www.arav.org.

On the home page of the ARAV Web site, you'll see a "Members" link. Click on that, and you'll next be asked to click on either a "United States" or "Worldwide" tab. Click on the appropriate one, and eventually you'll be able to narrow the choices down to the area closest to where you live. Once you arrive at the section that's close to your neck of the woods, up will pop a list of veterinarians who are members of the ARAV, along with their contact information. Look for vets in the list who appear to operate actual veterinary offices, and proceed from there.

illness, just to play it safe. For one thing, by the time your pet is exhibiting signs of illness, it has most likely already been sick for a while. In the wild, if an animal shows signs that it's sick, other animals recognize that it is weak, and therefore its life is in danger from them. Captive animals have retained this "hide that they are sick" trait, so by the time they do show signs of illness, there is no time to waste in making them well. So don't waste any!

Respiratory Problems

Your snake may be wheezing and having trouble breathing, or you may see a discharge or bubbles coming out from its nose. The affected animal may be breathing with its mouth open, have no energy, and may possibly have stopped eating.

Respiratory disease is very dangerous. A common cause is an enclosure that is too cold or too damp for your snake. (Yet

This gasping snake obviously needs to see a vet.

that result in respiratory problems. Snakes can also experience respiratory problems when they are kept on substrates that are too dusty. Because a snake crawls along the ground, if its substrate is dusty, the snake will inhale the dust. Avoid dusty substrates for this reason. (Pine shavings, for instance, are notoriously dusty, although other wood-based substrates, such as cypress bark and aspen shavings, are usually OK.)

another reason to do your research first so you make sure the enclosure is set for the right temperature and humidity!) Those conditions can lead to fungal and bacterial infections

If you notice any symptoms of respiratory problems, you should, in addition to making sure the substrate isn't too dusty, check the temperature of

This green tree python's mucous discharge indicates a respiratory problem. Warming up its cage may help, but antibiotics may also be necessary.

The patch of skin that remains stuck on this kingsnake after its shed may indicate a lack of necessary humidity in the snake's cage. Misting with warm water will help.

your pet's enclosure. Raising the overall enclosure temperature is usually a good idea. Keep your snake warm, and make an appointment for your pet to be examined by a veterinarian knowledgeable about reptiles if the condition persists. Antibiotics may be needed.

Abnormal Shedding

Like all reptiles, snakes shed their skins, and sometimes they suffer from an improper shed. If a snake doesn't shed its skin properly, old skin that is left attached can cause health problems.

Improper shedding usually means that you aren't taking care of your snake the right way. A common cause is a lack of humidity (moisture) in your snake's cage; in other words, the cage is too dry too much of the time. Humidity helps snakes shed their skins. Keep in mind that substrate can affect humidity, too. Some substrates, such as cypress mulch and bark, are moister than are others, such as sand. Moisture helps provide humidity.

If you notice patches of shed skin stuck to your pet, try misting it with warm water sprayed from a water bottle. If the skin doesn't come off by itself (always preferred), you may give a *very* gentle tug to help, which is usually OK. But don't tug hard or repeatedly if the skin doesn't come away easily because you could end up hurt-ing your pet. Mist with water as recommended, and soon the skin should be easily removed.

If you try raising the humidity of the cage by mist-ing it and the snake, and your pet still seems to be having problems shedding its skin, your next step is to (can you guess what I'm going to say?) take it to a vet. And don't mist with so much water that the cage is always wet; that can lead to respiratory problems.

Retained Eye Caps

Snakes that are not shedding properly may experience this con-dition. The spectacle or eye cap is the clear scale that covers a snake's eye. (You may remember reading about it in chapter 2.) Eye caps are shed periodically, just like the rest of a snake's skin. Sometimes, however, even when the rest of the skin is shed properly, the old eye cap may remain behind, stuck to your snake's eye.

Some people remove a stuck eye cap by moistening the eye cap and the surrounding area and *very, very gently* touching a piece of cellophane tape to the spectacle and *very, very* carefully lifting it away from the snake's head. If for any reason the shed eye cap is stubborn and doesn't come off easily right away, a visit to the veterinarian may be necessary.

Some keepers leave the retained eye cap alone if it doesn't appear to be bothering the snake in any way, to see whether it comes off by itself during the snake's next shed.

Internal Parasites

Think of internal parasites as little bugs or worms that can get inside your snake's body, sometimes arriving there inside the food your pet eats. Once they're in your snake's guts, the parasites can slowly sap the strength of your pet until it gets sick.

Usually, you can't tell your snake has internal parasites until it is actually acting sick, and by then it may be too late to save it. For this reason, as soon as you bring a new snake home, it's a good idea to have a **stool** sample (a piece of the snake's poop) examined by a vet, who will inspect it for parasites. If some are found, the veterinarian will prescribe medicine to help you get rid of them.

Wild-caught snakes are more likely to have internal parasites than are captive-bred ones—an excellent reason to always buy captive-bred snakes whenever possible—but any reptile can pick up parasites.

External Parasites

Internal parasites are inside your snake's body; external parasites are outside, on the skin.

Take a stool sample from a new snake to a vet to be examined for internal parasites. The small orange spheres on this rattlesnake fecal sample are tapeworm segments.

Here is a tick on a ball python. Ticks and mites may attach themselves to snakes that are kept in unclean enclosures. Examine new snakes closely for these pests.

These can include mites and ticks, two tiny bugs that can suck your snake's blood. There are other kinds of external parasites, too, but mites and ticks are the most common. Mites, especially, can attack snakes that are placed into unclean, contaminated cages in pet stores and at shipping facilities through which mite-infested snakes and lizards may have passed.

Sometimes parasites can invade your snake's cage by hitchhiking on a piece of wood you put in the cage or even on some of the live food, such as mice, you might offer your pets. If this happens, you have to not only treat your snake but also completely clean its cage and everything in it.

Even though external parasites can be very small, you can usually see them when they're on your snake. Mites, for instance, look like teensy red dots scurrying around on your snake's body and clustered beneath its scales. Snakes that have mites will sometimes scratch themselves on objects inside their cages.

Although it's best to take a mite-infected snake to the veterinarian, some people prefer

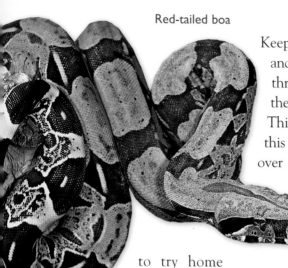

Red-tailed boa

Keepers soak their hands in oil and let their snakes slither through their hands, coating the snakes' bodies with oil. This smothers mites. Again, this has to be done repeatedly over a few weeks to eliminate any mites that hatch in between treatments.

These home remedies are not to try home remedies that have been used to treat snake mites over the years. These include holding your snake underwater—except for its nose so it can breathe—for several minutes a day. Mites will drown and fall of your snake. Mite eggs, however, are not affected. That means you have to repeat this procedure over the course of a few weeks, so you can drown recently hatched mites. The problem here is that the snake could struggle while under the water, possibly injuring itself. Besides that, you can imagine how stressful the dunking experience would be for your pet.

Another home fix uses oil (vegetable, olive, or baby oil).

foolproof. If you see anything weird on your snake's skin—whether it's something moving or any kind of lump or bump that doesn't look right—take your animal to a veterinarian. External parasites can be removed, and sometimes when a snake sheds its skin, the parasites are shed along with it. But the longer these beasties are on your pet, the worse it is for the snake. A vet will help you get rid of them.

Burns

Snakes don't feel pain the way we do: they're wired differently. If you placed your body on a very hot surface, you would jerk it away. Snakes, however, may not do that. No one is quite sure why, but they may maintain contact with an extra-hot surface until they get burned, and some can be burned quite badly. Every once in a while, snakes burn themselves on improperly placed or used heating devices. Hot rocks, for instance, which look like rocks and heat up when they're plugged in, can sometimes burn a snake if they malfunction or if their thermostats are set too high. Other times, a snake may come into contact with a heat lamp and get burned.

Be sure your snake cannot come into direct contact with any kind of heating element you are using to keep the enclosure warm.

Accidents

Because your pet snakes are alive and moving (at least, I hope they are), they can sometimes have accidents. If you stack some rocks in the cage, for instance, be sure they cannot fall on top of your pet and hurt it, especially if the snake is pushing beneath the rocks at the time. (Consider using silicone glue to attach rocks to the bottom of the cage and each other to prevent them from falling over. Have an adult help you, if necessary.)

If your snake ever has an accident and gets hurt, a vet should examine it and decide on the best type of treatment to get your pet back to tip-top condition.

Reptile veterinarians definitely get to see some interesting patients!

Prey Bites

If you feed your snakes living prey items, the prey may fight back. This is one reason why many snake keepers prefer to feed their snakes previously killed prey—plus, if the prey has been frozen and thawed, there is less chance of something, such as an internal parasite, being passed from the prey to the snake.

If you feed live rodents to your snake, never ever leave one unattended or in your snake's enclosure overnight. The mouse or rat may attack your snake while it's sleeping, injuring your pet severely. I've seen some pretty gross photos of snakes that were chewed on by their intended meals. Always remove uneaten prey items, and try offering them again later. If your snake does suffer severe bites from its prey, have a vet examine it for signs of infection.

Impactions

Impactions, also known as intestinal blockages, were mentioned briefly in the substrate section in chapter 4. They can result from your snake's accidentally eating its substrate. A snake with an impaction will often

A live rat was left in this python's cage overnight, and the results are not pretty. Never leave a living rodent in your snake's cage unattended—some prey will fight back!

This python is bloated from an impaction that resulted after the snake ate a towel that was kept in its cage! Be sure to always use a proper substrate.

stop feeding, and it won't be able to go to the bathroom. An impaction can kill your snake if not treated by a qualified veterinarian. Surgery may be necessary to get your snake well.

To avoid impactions, inspect your snake's cage for any possible causes (corncob bedding has been reported to be especially problematic with impactions), and change the environment accordingly. Consider feeding your snake in a separate cage, one that doesn't have any substrate on the bottom, because the most likely time for your snake to accidentally eat some substrate is when it's feeding.

Mouth Rot

Mouth rot is a bacterial infection that settles in a snake's mouth and gums. As a result, they can become severely affected, and advanced cases may lead to the snake's mouth becoming deformed and swollen, with whitish or yellowish pus. A snake with mouth rot will often stop eating. If your snake has mouth rot, take it to a veterinarian, where its mouth will likely be swabbed with medication.

Bacteria breed in unclean environments, so mouth rot can often be avoided if you

Many health problems in pet snakes are caused by their being kept in unclean conditions. If you keep your snake's cage clean, including removing poop as soon as you see it, you'll go a long way toward keeping your snake healthy.

Poop removal should be kept in mind when you're choosing the substrate for your snake's enclosure: choose one that allows easy spot cleaning. For instance, if you use cypress mulch or sand and notice some snake poop on top of it, it's easy to remove just the soiled portion and replace it with clean substrate.

If you use reptile carpet or artificial turf for a substrate, you can't spot clean. Instead, have some clean pieces ready at all times. Then when your reptile has gone to the bathroom, you can remove the entire dirtied piece of carpeting and replace it right away with a clean piece. Clean the soiled piece, and set it aside to dry for future use.

Water bowls can easily become filthy. Some snakes enjoy lying in their water bowls, and they will also go to the bathroom in them. Replace the water and clean the bowl at least once every day—more often, if needed.

simply keep your snake's cage clean at all times. (See the "Clean Means Healthy" box.)

Inclusion Body Disease

Inclusion body disease is a viral infection that affects boids (boas and pythons) but not colubrids (such as kingsnakes and corn snakes). Although internal organs such as the spleen and kidneys can be affected, the disease primarily attacks the central nervous system.

A snake that has inclusion body disease may become partially paralyzed and not be able to crawl properly or to strike at

This boa constrictor is "stargazing"—pulling up its head and neck—which may be a sign of inclusion body disease. The snake should be quarantined immediately.

its food. It may flip over onto its back and be unable to right itself. A snake with this disease may also be found **stargazing**, which means its head and neck are involuntarily pulled up, forcing the snake to look upward. It may vomit, it may not shed properly, and its body shape may wither away.

Inclusion body disease is still somewhat mysterious. No one's certain what causes it. Some veterinarians believe a particular mite plays a role. Sadly, right now there is no cure for it, and it's recommended that boas and pythons that

have inclusion body disease be euthanized ("put to sleep").

Inclusion body disease is highly contagious, and some snakes showing no signs of the disease may be carriers that could pass it on to other snakes in a collection. This is why it's important to **quarantine** new snakes before adding any to an existing collection. (See the "Quarantine New Snakes" box.)

Regurgitation

To regurgitate means to throw up. Snakes may do it for different reasons. Stress may cause a snake to throw up, so be sure to help your snake avoid stress. Giving it places to hide, as described in chapter 4, really helps a snake feel safe and secure.

Handling your snake too soon after it's eaten might cause your pet to regurgitate. Just as it's advisable for you to wait awhile to go swimming after eating a meal, you should wait awhile to handle your snake after it has eaten.

Regurgitation can also be a sign of serious disease, such as inclusion body disease. Take your snake to a veterinarian for an examination if it throws up often.

Owning pets means being willing to make them well if they're sick. This means taking them to a vet. This can sometimes be expensive, but isn't your snake worth it?

Quarantine New Snakes

To quarantine a new snake means to keep it in a separate cage away from other snakes rather than placing it anywhere near snakes you already have. By keeping the new arrival separate for several days (at least until you can have your vet check it and tell you it isn't sick), you will avoid the possibility that it will contaminate the healthy snakes in your collection. Quarantine is especially important for new pythons and boas because of inclusion body disease, which is incurable and fatal.

A snake may regurgitate if it's handled too soon after eating.

Salmonella

Although pet reptiles—snakes to a degree, but especially turtles—have been linked to cases of *Salmonella* (pronounced sal-meh-NEH-la), the number of people who get sick from this because of their pet reptiles is small. *Salmonella* is a bacteria that causes a disease called **salmonellosis**, which can make you sick to your stomach, give you diarrhea, and cause other unpleasant side effects. It's most likely to affect very young kids, senior citizens, and people who have weak immune systems.

The key to avoiding salmonellosis is to keep everything clean. Whenever you handle your pets or anything that's inside their cages, wash your hands thoroughly with a disinfectant soap. The same goes for objects used with your snakes, such as water bowls and cage decorations. Wash up very thoroughly, and never handle any of your animals or their supplies in areas where they could come into contact with your family's food, kitchen sinks, and bathtubs. Anytime you're working with your snakes or any of your snake supplies and equipment, clean up your work area completely. Don't give *Salmonella* even the teensiest chance to contaminate anything.

CHAPTER 9

Dos and Don'ts for Snake Owners

K eep the following ten dos and ten don'ts in mind if you plan to keep a snake. All twenty are covered in more detail elsewhere in this book. I hope that you use them to make your experiences happy ones and that you and your snake (or snakes) are together for many years to come!

Boa constrictor

Remember that snakes are born escape artists, so you should always be certain your snake's enclosure is completely escape-proof.

Do read a lot and conduct research before buying a snake.

Do buy healthy snakes, especially captive-bred specimens.

Do be sure to provide hiding places inside your snake's enclosure.

Do provide the proper levels of heat and humidity to keep your snake healthy.

Do feed your snakes only clean and healthy prey.

Do keep your pet's enclosure clean (especially the substrate and the water in your snake's water bowl).

Do be on the lookout for any signs of illness, and take your snake to a veterinarian at the first sign of illness.

Do everything in your power to make your snake's enclosure escape-proof.

Do remember to always wash your hands after handling your snake and anything that may have been in its enclosure.

Do respect other people's feelings toward snakes, especially if they are afraid of them.

No matter how pretty or interesting-looking a snake may be, and even if it's very inexpensive, never buy one on impulse. Know what it is and how to care for it first.

Don't buy any animal on impulse.

Don't buy a snake without knowing how big it will get.

Don't get any pet unless you are absolutely sure you can take care of it for as long as it will live (this is a *long* time for some snakes!).

Don't bring home a sick animal thinking you'll make it well.

Don't take your snakes outside where they may come into contact with strangers.

Don't keep snakes on dusty pine or cedar shavings.

Don't forget to provide a heat gradient for your snake.

Don't handle your snake too soon after it has eaten.

Don't keep kingsnakes with other snakes, unless you want the other snakes to be eaten!

Don't leave any live rodents in with a snake overnight or otherwise unattended.

And last but not least, here's one never:
***Never** stop learning about snakes!*

Glossary

arboreal: living among branches

boid: a nonvenomous snake, such as a boa, that kills its prey by crushing it

camouflage: to hide or disguise oneself to blend in with one's environment

captive-bred: a reptile that is born from parents kept in captivity

captivity: kept in a cage to prevent escape; living in captivity is the opposite of living in the wild or in nature

clutch: a group of eggs

cold-blooded: having a body temperature that goes up or down with the temperature of the environment; an ectotherm

colubrid: a snake from the Colubridae family of mostly nonvenomous snakes

constrictor: a snake that coils around its prey to suffocate it

ectothermic: see *cold-blooded*

endangered: an animal with only a small number of its kind left in the wild

fuzzies: young rodents that are starting to grow hair

habitat: the specific area in which an animal naturally lives

heat gradient: see *thermal gradient*

herp: a nickname for a reptile; comes from *herpetology*, the study of reptiles and amphibians

herping: a word hobbyists use to describe looking for reptiles in nature

hibernate: to be in a resting state in which there is almost no activity

hobbyist: a person who keeps reptiles as pets and studies them for fun

husbandry: the care and management of, in this context, reptiles

impaction: a blockage in the snake's intestines

keel: a raised ridge

morph: an animal with a special color or pattern

ontogenetic color change: color change that occurs as a snake becomes an adult

ophidiophobia: a fear of snakes

oviparous: producing eggs that develop and hatch outside the body

ovoviviparous: producing eggs that develop and hatch inside the body

pelagic: living in the open ocean

pinky mice (pinkies): newborn mice that get this nickname because their hairless bodies are pink

prey items: food for snakes

quarantine: to separate an animal from other animals

range: the area of a country (or even specific parts of a region or state) where a reptile can be found in the wild

regurgitate: throw up food

reptiles: animals from the class Reptilia, a group of cold-blooded, air-breathing animals that move on their bellies or

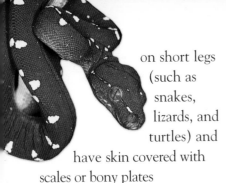

on short legs (such as snakes, lizards, and turtles) and have skin covered with scales or bony plates

road cruising: nighttime driving to look for snakes on paved roads

salmonellosis: a disease caused by *Salmonella* bacteria that humans can catch from reptiles; symptoms include upset stomach and diarrhea in humans

spurs: clawlike projections on either side of a male boa or python's vent (its butt), the remnants of the legs of the animals that became snakes

stargazing: when a snake's head and neck are involuntarily pulled up, forcing the snake to look upward

stool: poop

substrate: the material you put on the bottom of a reptile's cage

tease-feeding: jiggling the prey item so it looks as if it's alive, to get the snake to eat

thermal gradient: the temperature range you create by placing heating elements on only one side of the cage; allows the cold-blooded reptile to move either to the warm side or to the cool side of the cage to reach its desired body temperature

thermoregulating: changing body temperature by moving from a warm place to a cool place, or from a cool place to a warm place

ultraviolet (UV) light: a type of light that humans can't see

venomous: poisonous

wild-caught: captured in the wild

Recommended Reading

Reptiles Magazine
A monthly publication covering herps from A to Z.
The Web site provides useful care tips as well as links to breeders,
photo galleries, and message boards.
http://www.reptilesmagazine.com
PO Box 6050 • Mission Viejo, CA 92690

The following two field guides have been around for many years
and are still favorites of many herpers in the United States. Both
are available in paperback and are part of the popular Peterson
Field Guides series.

Conant, Roger, and Joseph Collins. *A Field Guide to
Reptiles and Amphibians: Eastern and Central North America*.
4th ed. Houghton Mifflin, 1998.

Stebbins, Robert. *A Field Guide to Western Reptiles*. 3rd ed.
Houghton Mifflin, 2003.

Photo Credits

COVER
Front cover (main image and boxes): Paul Freed.

FRONT MATTER
Title and Contents: Paul Freed.

CHAPTER 1
4, 9: Paul Freed. **5 (top and bottom), 6–8 (top):** Bill Love/Blue Chameleon Ventures. **8 (bottom):** Victor Habbick Visions.

CHAPTER 2
10: Bill Love/Blue Chameleon Ventures. **11 (top), 12 (top), 15, 17 (top):** Photos.com. **11 (bottom), 25:** James E. Gerholdt. **12 (bottom):** David Northcott. **13, 16–17 (bottom), 19, 22–24:** Paul Freed. **14:** Don Swerida. **18:** Philippe de Vosjoli. **20, 21 (bottom):** Zig Leszczynski. **21 (top):** Cynthia A. Delaney. **21 (middle):** Jim Merli.

CHAPTER 3
26: David Northcott. **27, 33–34, 36–40, 43:** Paul Freed. **28–29, 35, 45:** Photos.com. **30, 42, 44:** Bill Love/Blue Chameleon Ventures. **31:** Shutterstock.com.

CHAPTER 4
46: David Northcott. **47 (top and bottom), 49–50 (top and bottom, both pages), 51, 52 (top), 53–57, 59 (top):** Paul Freed. **48:** Philippe de Vosjoli. **52 (bottom):** Bill Love/Blue ChameleonVentures. **58 (bottom), 59 (bottom):** Photos.com.

CHAPTER 5
60: Gerold and Cindy Merker. **61–63, 65:** Paul Freed. **64:** Bill Love/Blue Chameleon Ventures.

CHAPTER 6
66, 72–74, 75 (top and bottom), 76–77, 79: Paul Freed. **67, 69–71:** Bill Love/Blue Chameleon Ventures. **78:** Gerold and Cindy Merker.

CHAPTER 7
80–81, 82 (bottom), 83, 84 (top and bottom), 86–87, 88 (top and bottom), 91, 94: Paul Freed. **82 (top), 89:** Bill Love/Blue Chameleon Ventures. **90:** R. D. Bartlett. **93:** Photos.com. **92, 95:** Allen Blake Sheldon.

CHAPTER 8
96–97, 99 (bottom), 100, 110: Paul Freed. **99 (top), 102, 105–107, 109:** John Rossi. **103:** Bill Love/Blue Chameleon Ventures. **104:** David Northcott. **111:** Photos.com

CHAPTER 9
112: Paul Freed. **113–114:** Bill Love/Blue Chameleon Ventures.

GLOSSARY
116, 117 (top): Paul Freed. **115, 117 (bottom):** Bill Love/Blue Chameleon Ventures.

ABOUT THE AUTHOR
120: Sandy Quinn. Whitesmoke/pastel/woma ball python courtesy of Vida Preciosa International, Inc.

About the Author

Russ Case is the group editor of the monthly magazines *Reptiles*, *Aquarium Fish International*, and *Freshwater and Marine Aquarium* as well as the annual magazines *Reptiles USA*, *Aquarium USA*, and *Marine Fish and Reef USA*. He lives in Southern California and has been a reptile and amphibian enthusiast since he was a small child exploring the wilds of suburban New Jersey in the 1960s. Lizards are his favorite herps, but he's also very fond of snakes, turtles, and amphibians, and he has kept many different types over the years.

Snakes Stickers

Can you find where to place these in the book?